The following is a ~~sample of the testimonial~~ received on ~~the~~ *Best Deal* series:

Many Realtors® might put this down as too elementary, but I wish all my clients would review the simple steps provided here so they could learn to be an effective part of the teamwork it takes to fulfill their dreams. This book has the exact things most buyers and sellers need to know but are afraid to ask.

—John Foltz, President, Realty Executives

This book is a wonderful road map for the ever-confusing world of real estate. It's like having your own personal coach in a box.

—Melissa Giovagnoli, Author, best-selling book, *Networlding: Building Relationships and Opportunities for Success* and *How to Grow a Great Business and Power Network*

The real estate world is constantly changing, so anyone who is even considering buying [or selling] property of any kind should first get a copy of this easy-to-read and straightforward book. [It] demonstrates how valuable a good real estate professional can be—and further—how to select the right one. Smart real estate agents will also read the book to ensure their [clients] are receiving the service and the expertise they deserve.

—Dave Liniger, Co-founder and Chairman of RE/MAX

This book should be required reading for all Realtors® and for anyone serious about real estate.

—Peter J. McLaughlin, author of *CatchFire: A Seven Step Program to Ignite Energy, Defuse Stress and Power Boost Your Performance*

I read your book and I think it is eminently readable. That's one thing most such publications intended for the public fail to be. There is a lot of good information in it that consumers can benefit from.

—Edwin J. Ricketts, Deputy Commissioner of the Arizona Department of Real Estate

. . . In life it seems you don't get what you deserve, you get what you negotiate, and *How to Make Your REALTOR® Get You the Best Deal* gives you the necessary tools it takes to be in the best possible position to negotiate in real estate. My hat is off to Jenny, Ken, and their national consortium.

> —Mike Barnett, VP Technology of Internet Crusade (an organization providing communication training to Realtors® nationwide)

In this book . . . several profoundly successful real estate agents have provided a simple guide through the often dark and confusing waters of home buying or selling. They demonstrate the impact of recent changes in the law and how those changes can affect the quality of representation one receives. Read this book and you will learn how to screen, select, and then use your Realtor® in a way that *Gets You the Best Deal*.

> —Steve Largent, U.S. Congressional Representative, Oklahoma

This is a ground-breaking work for home sellers. It is not only a quick read, but it puts in layman's terms the language of real estate. This book will do more to empower the home seller than anything else in print. I strongly recommend you buy this book before you even consider putting your home on the market.

> —Michael E. Houtari, Corporate Attorney

Get the Best Deal When Selling Your Home

San Francisco
Bay Area Edition

Get the Best Deal When Selling Your Home

San Francisco Bay Area Edition

by Ira Serkes, Samia Morgan,
Pete Sabine,
and
Ken Deshaies

Gabriel Publications

Gabriel Publications
14340 Addison St. #101
Sherman Oaks, California 91423
Visit our website at www.GabrielBooks.com
Or call: (800) 940-2622

Get the Best Deal When Selling Your Home San Francisco Bay Area Edition
Ira Serkes, Samia Morgan, Pete Sabine, and Ken Deshaies
ISBN-13: 978-1-891689-87-1
ISBN-10: 1-891689-87-8
Library of Congress Catalog Card Number: 2004105168
Typography: SDS Design, info@sds-design.com
Cover Design: Dale Schroeder, SDS Design
Editors: David Robman and Kate Shaffar
Publisher: Gabriel Publications, Simon Rawlinson, V.P.
Distributed by: Partners Publishers Group

Printed in the United States of America.

Contents

Section I
Selling Your Home: The Basics

Section II
Buying Your Next Home

Appendices

Acknowledgements by Ira & Carol Serkes

In the acknowledgements to my book, *How to Buy a House in California* I wrote: At 20 I had my entire life planned; at 40 I had no idea what opportunities lay ahead, and at 50 I didn't realize how prescient I was at 40. Thankfully, more years have passed, and I know that the best adventures of *la dolce vita* lay ahead! As I write this from our sofa in **Casa Serkes**, our Spanish-Med home in Berkeley's Thousand Oaks neighborhood, it's important to give thanks to many people.

First and foremost to my parents, **Max and Adele Serkes** whose ethical standards always made it easy for me to know how to "do the right thing." My mother Adele died of long life while I was writing this book, but her spirit lives on. Carol and I think of her every time we step into **Casita Adela**.

To my wife, **Carol**, who taught me the difference between a house and a home.

To **Ken Deshaies**, who provided the inspiration to write a book dedicated to home sellers.

To **Rennie Gabriel** and **David Robman**, Publisher and Editor, as well as **Samia Morgan** and **Pete Sabine**, co-authors, whose patience allowed us to create a book we're all very proud of.

To **John & Ellen Pinto** (between the three of us, we have The Bronx, Brooklyn, and Queens covered) for showing us how to live *la dolce vita* (see paragraph 3).

Carol once said that, "Ira has lived long enough for the technology to catch up with the ideas in his head." And so, I owe a big debt of gratitude to **Steve Jobs** for making the "Insanely Great" Macintosh Computer, and to **Al Gore**, for inventing the Internet. Without their contributions, I'd probably still be trying to figure out how to balance a DEC PDP 8 computer and ASR 110 baud Teletype onto my lap.

Acknowledgments by Samia Morgan

Thank you to my co-authors, **Ira Serkes** and **Pete Sabine**, for the collaborative work we did together and for keeping one another motivated.

I would like to thank my husband, **Tom** and children **Sami, Jack**, and **Chantal**, for their support during this process and for their patience while I grew my business over the last decades. My kids grew up with me in the business, had to deal with me being gone a lot on evenings, weekends, to conferences and seminars, and often working while on vacation.

To my parents, without whom I would not be in this country or had a career in real estate. **Sami** and **Nadia Marcos** immigrated to the United States in 1969 and sacrificed their lifestyle and comfort for our future. My parents asked me if I would like to invest in real estate with them while I was in college. They borrowed $5,000 from the local credit union and I borrowed it from them. From then on, we purchased additional properties, improved them and rolled them into other properties. *You are never too young to invest.* My parents taught me the value of hard work and the importance of good work ethics. They are the most generous and wonderful parents a child can ever have and I thank them every day for bringing us to the United States so that we could partake of the opportunities made available to us.

I would especially like to thank my staff. **Roberta Goodwin**, a friend and client who has been working with me for a number of years is great at keeping me focused. **Kim Hughes**, my virtual assistant, for all her hard work across the miles. Kim keeps my projects on track so that I can maximize my time with clients and help them achieve their real estate goals.

Real estate is my third career and my most rewarding one. I have been fortunate enough to form lifelong relationships with a lot of my clients and have serviced their needs and those of their families. I would like to acknowledge them here as well, and thank them for their continued support.

I would like to thank the **San Mateo County Association of REALTORS®** for helping me to see the value of being involved and nudging me into leadership. Thank you to **David Zigal** who is one of the first people I met in real estate and who has helped me grow into the business. It was my honor to serve with David on the Board of Directors of our association.

I gracious thank you to my colleague, **Cheryl Scott-Daniels**, a premier Realtor® in Westport, Connecticut. Cheryl and I entered the business at the same time and had similar backgrounds. While across the county, we constantly share ideas and new techniques. We met at a **National Association of REALTORS®** conference and have been soul mates ever since.

Thank you to **Nina Cottrell, Dick Dillingham, Mike Brodie,** and **Pat Zaby**, leaders and great role models at the **Certified Residential Specialist (CRS)** organization, an affiliate of the National Association of REALTORS®. My involvement in CRS has helped me grow and become a better person and a better Realtor®.

I would like to also thank **Howard Brinton** and the **Star Power** organization for giving me the tools to improve my skills and succeed at a higher level.

Thank you to **Allen Hainge** for founding the **CyberStars™** group and for his leadership in helping agents improve the integration of technology in their business.

Last, but not least, **Gary Keller** and **Joe Williams**, for co-founding **Keller Williams®** Realty International. Keller Williams has provided their agents with a new model for real estate offices and have launched a tremendous amount of educational tools to support them. **Mo**

Anderson, Mark Willis, Dave Jenks, and **Mary Tenant** are awesome leaders within that organization. I thank them all for their constant renewal of ideas and energy into the company.

Acknowledgments by Pete Sabine

This book is a tribute to the real estate profession and what I consider to be the most rewarding career I could have chosen to foster my personal and professional growth. Selling residential real estate is a "people business." Every transaction is different because the people involved and their related goals and circumstances are different.

I have been blessed with hundreds of opportunities to assist my clients realize their dreams and build wealth through buying and selling real estate. I offer my deepest gratitude to all of my past clients who put their faith and trust in me to assist them with their real estate transactions. This book is also my opportunity to offer something of value by sharing my trade secrets and lessons learned to benefit my future clients.

There are many people I want to acknowledge for their support over the past two decades of my real estate career.

To my father, **Gerald Ortland**, for sharing his expertise and enthusiasm in encouraging me to enter into the real estate profession at the young age of 26 years. My dad helped me through the challenges of getting my career off the ground when I became frustrated and discouraged in those early days of selling real estate.

To **David Cobo, C.E.O.** of **Prudential California Real Estate**. David took a chance by hiring me when I had no experience selling real estate. He provided access to his vast depth of real estate experience as well as assisting me with the purchase of my first home.

To **Joe Stumpf** and the **By Referral Only** organization. Joe taught me the virtues of taking better care of my existing clients and to foster long-term relationships beyond the closing date of the real estate transaction. Through implementation of his teachings and

10

philosophies, I became "relationship" oriented instead of "transaction" oriented with my real estate practice. I have developed a referral-based business with over 80 percent of my transactions coming from repeat clients and referrals.

To my family and friends, who stood by me for all these years and made many comprises for my unpredictable work schedule. With their support and understanding, I was able to balance my professional life with my personal life.

I hope this book will provide valuable insight into the realities of buying and selling real estate in the San Francisco Bay Area.

Acknowledgments by Ken Deshaies

There are those without whom this book would not have been written and they deserve more than the recognition given here. Their faith in me, at times, exceeded my own.

My publisher, **Rennie Gabriel**, and I have formed a partnership of ideas that has done several things. My first book, *How to Make Your Realtor Get You the Best Deal*, has been much more successful than either of us had ever imagined. As a consequence, we have both been able to bring a semblance of understanding and self help to thousands of consumers across this great land. We have also enabled dozens of Realtors® to participate in getting out the message. In the process, we have become great friends and cohorts. Not everyone will agree with our methods, but then, we have not been seeking agreement. What we have done, is to empower people on both sides of the real estate purchasing process, including the professionals who work with, and represent them.

My good friend, a fellow REALTOR® and e-PRO, **Mollie Wasserman**. Mollie is a true pioneer in the area of real estate and the Internet and we are truly fortunate that she was willing to provide a special chapter for us on this topic. This is a very important subject in today's real estate transactions, and we urge all of our readers to make sure they are prepared to deal with the benefits and limitations of the Internet.

Davida Sims and **David Robman** contributed so much to this manuscript, and their efforts are more than appreciated.

Allen Hainge, founder of the CyberStars, an elite group of Realtors® from around the country and abroad who can not only prove experiential success with the use of technology in this business, but have agreed to be teaching professionals with Allen. Allen welcomed me with open arms into this wonderful organization several years ago, and has become a good friend and mentor ever since.

John Beldock, founder of EcoBroker International, a school for training real estate professionals about energy efficient homes, for his valuable contributions to this book.

The hundreds of clients with whom my wife, **Mary** and I have worked with through the years have provided the fodder and the inspiration for this book. So many of them have become good friends in the process, that our family is huge.

Patricia McDade, founder and inspirational leader of The Entrepreneurial Edge, provided the initial kick in the proverbial rear to get me to do that over which I'd procrastinated for so long.

All four of us would like to thank **Mary Pope Handy** of Silicon Valley, California for contributing much of the section on California Agency and Disclosures (www.popehandy. com or 800-555-1212).

"You don't end up in the grave. You end up in the hearts of the people you have touched."

Disclaimer

We've tried, we really have. We have attempted to ensure that everything said here is accurate and relevant. But laws change, circumstances vary, home prices and interest rates change and there is always the possibility for error. There may be mistakes, both typographical and in content, and the information was current only up to the printing date. Using the guidance offered here, along with your selection of a competent real estate professional, you should feel confident in purchasing or selling real estate. This text should be used only as a general guide and not as the ultimate source of real estate information. If your situation is complicated by any of a myriad of factors, such as the property being a business, farm or ranch, or if it has soil, septic tank, well, or title problems, we recommend you consult with a Realtor® who specializes in that area. We are not providing any accounting, legal, or tax advice in this book. We recommend that you hire an attorney or other appropriate professional who can assist with the specifics involved in any legal or tax matter. The purpose of this book is to educate and entertain. The publisher and authors shall have neither liability nor responsibility to any person or entity with respect to any loss or damage caused, directly or indirectly, by the information contained in this book. If you do not wish to be bound by the above, you may return the book for a full refund.

About gender usage: In order to avoid numerous grammatical messes and to make the reading flow better, we have chosen to make this book as gender neutral as possible. We have used *they* and *their,* even for one person, instead of *he or she, his and hers,* and so on.

About the term *Realtor*®: This is a registered trademark of the National Association of REALTORS® (NAR), and anyone who uses that term as part of their professional identity must be a member not only of the NAR, but also of their local and state associations. We always encourage both buyers and sellers to seek out the services of a Realtor® when possible. However, even though we recommend the use of a Realtor®, we know there are many small communities in the country where there are no Realtors®. Often throughout this book we refer to "agent," "licensee," "real estate salesperson," "broker," and so forth. We do this because anyone who holds a real estate sales license must abide by laws, which we will cover in Chapter 11. These laws apply to *all* real estate agents in the United States, not just Realtors®. To make the text easier to read you will see the term *Realtor*® used showing the registration mark and lower case letters after the initial capital *R*. Please see Chapter 2 for a more complete explanation of this designation.

Again, please consult with a professional in your state based on your situation. You can also reach the author directly through the contact information provided near the beginning and at the end of the book. Also, feel free to contact the author for a referral to a Realtor® in your area.

Introduction by the Publisher

For many people, their home is the largest investment they will make in their lives. This book is designed to help you, as a homeowner, get the greatest return when you're ready to sell that investment. But right now your house is your home. It is where you shelter yourself from the outside world, where you raise children, bond with your mate, and express your individuality. When it comes time to sell your house (and your home) your thinking has to shift from a personal statement of who you are, or your values, to an investment vehicle that will attract the greatest audience. It needs to appeal to the specific demographics of your potential buyer. Remember, the prospective buyer will be comparing your house and home to all the others on the market that fit their needs, wants, and desires.

A small change, or addition to your house can add thousands of dollars of profit to you, while spending money in the wrong way can actually cost you thousands more. You will see many examples in the following pages, but here is one example: If you spent $25,000 on a swimming pool, you would be lucky to get half of it back in the increased value of your home. In addition, you would pay additional property taxes, utility bills, and cleaning and maintenance costs over the life of the swimming pool.

Unfortunately, many people think they can save thousands of dollars by selling a home by themselves. When selling a home, the requirements of disclosure, compensation, marketing and legality are becoming more and more complicated. If it looks easy, that's proof you've been working with an agent who is competent and doing their job. Selling a home "by owner" is just as unwise. How can the experience of selling one, or even a few homes, match the experience of a professional who does it day in and day out?

A study conducted by the National Association of REALTORS® determined that people who sold their homes themselves received 21 percent less than comparable homes where the owner used the services of a Realtor®. Another way of looking at it is to recognize that avoiding the services of an agent and saving about 6 percent, or less, on commissions may cost 21 percent of the sales price that could be received.

If you were a homebuyer you might think that you're paying 21 percent more when you buy a home through a Realtor® instead of going directly to an owner. But based on national figures, the initial sale price an owner sets is well above the appropriate market price of comparable homes. In most situations a buyer working directly with a seller, with no agent support, will not know if a home is under- or overpriced. They won't know what inspector to hire to evaluate the integrity of the structure and systems, nor will they understand the responsibilities and liabilities of the other party. In many cases they will not know what forms and/or wording will provide the best protection if something goes wrong. And there are a host of other items that provide safeguards that both buyer and seller may not be aware of. This book will cover all of these issues, and more.

In this book Ira Serkes, Samia Morgan, and Pete Sabine have teamed up with Ken Deshaies to expose the secrets of how Realtors® are able to get more money for home sellers, as well as sell homes faster than those who attempt to do it alone. The authors not only share their own experiences, but have interviewed leading Realtors® from around the country in order to gather their best ideas and practices. If you are looking to buy your first home, this book can also give you invaluable insights into finding the right home, financing the purchase while saving thousands of dollars in the process.

About the Authors

IRA AND CAROL SERKES are local RE/MAX Realtors® who have lived in Berkeley, California for over 25 years. They specialize in helping nice folks buy and sell wonderful homes in Berkeley, Albany, Kensington, El Cerrito, Piedmont, Oakland, and Emeryville's most livable neighborhoods. Ira's designations include Certified Residential Specialist (CRS), Graduate REALTORS® Institute (GRI), Accredited Buyer Representative (ABR), Certified Internet Real Estate Professional (e-PRO 500), and Seniors Real Estate Specialist (SRES). Carol holds the Certified Residential Specialist (CRS) and the Graduate Realtors® Institute (GRI) designations.

The BerkeleyHomes.com website is personally created, developed, and maintained by Ira and Carol, two working, full-time (and then some) Realtors® with extensive experience on the ins and outs of buying and selling an East Bay home. Ira is coauthor of Nolo Press' best selling book, *How To Buy a House in California*, now in its 10th edition. He is an Allen F. Hainge CyberStar of the year.

Ira grew up in The Bronx, graduated from the Bronx High School Of Science, received a BS in chemical engineering from Cooper Union, and a MS in chemical engineering from the University of Massachusetts in Amherst. He worked for ten years as an engineer for Chevron Research, and holds two patents for his research. He teaches Realtors® how to use computers to better serve their clients.

Carol was born in Newcastle-On-Tyne, England, so she speaks American English reasonably well and now is a proud American citizen. She is trained as a paralegal and has been affiliated with one of the Bay Area's largest law firms. Carol has been an avid gardener in the past, but now really enjoys reading. They're the British - Yiddish team!

We really enjoy being with each other, eating out, going to movies, eating spicy foods, riding on steam trains, photographing Art Deco buildings and traveling (Ira thinks that any place in the great outdoors is fine as long as it's not more than a mile or two from the car and within an hour or two from a decent cup of coffee). Their many cats keep them company when they find themselves at home.

To Reach Ira and Carol Serkes
RE/MAX Executive
(510) 526-6668; Toll Free (800) 887-6668
Serkes@BerkeleyHomes.com
BerkeleyHomes.com
or
see page 158

SAMIA MORGAN, a licensed real estate broker, community leader, wife and mother, knows how important good organization is in everyday life—and in closing real estate transactions. She's detail-oriented and focused on keeping her clients completely informed. Recognized for her outstanding real estate achievements, you can be confident of Samia's commitment to your satisfaction—in fact she guarantees it.

Samia's designations include Certified Residential Specialist (CRS), the highest designation awarded by the National Association of REALTORS®, Accredited Buyer Representative (ABR), and the Leadership Training Graduate (LTG).

Samia prides herself on using the latest technology to assist her clients in their home search and making the transaction as seamless as possible. With a 24-hour voice mail system, a cell phone, and email. She is always easy to reach. If you, or someone you know, would like to sell your Bay Area home as quickly and easily as possible, and/or find a home that truly satisfies your needs while receiving outstanding service, call Samia. You'll be glad you did. Samia Morgan will be your real estate professional for life.

To Reach Samia S. Morgan, Inc.
Direct Line: (650) 352-5220; Toll free (800) 493-1715
samia@samiamorgan.com
move2ca.com
or
see page 158

PETE SABINE is a full-time Real Estate Consultant specializing in residential property sales since 1985. Pete brings together an extensive background in sales, marketing, negotiation, relocation, and construction with buying and selling strategies focused on delivering quality services, expertise, and innovative solutions for his clients. Over the course of his real estate career, Pete has successfully completed more than 500 real estate transactions in Contra Costa County. Following an advanced study in listing, selling, investment, and taxes, Pete earned his designation as a Certified Residential Specialist (CRS). He is a graduate of the REALTORS® Institute of California, a member of the Contra Costa Association of REALTORS®, the California Association of REALTORS®, the National Association of REALTORS,® and the Residential Sales Council.

Pete is a consistent top producing real estate broker and a member of the RE/MAX Platinum Club. The Platinum Club membership is awarded to the top 5 percent of the 96,856 RE/MAX agents located in 52 countries worldwide.

Since founding his real estate team, Pete and his team are focused on delivering a new industry standard of quality services, depth of expertise, and innovative solutions. Members of his team are passionate about empowering their clients to achieve their desired results.

Pete has resided in many Contra Costa County cities since 1963, including Pleasant Hill, Walnut Creek, Lafayette, Orinda, Martinez, and Concord. Prior to becoming a successful Real Estate consultant, Pete was a general contractor specializing in residential construction in various Contra Costa County communities. Over the years, Pete has actively supported the community as a volunteer with the Contra Costa Consolidated Fire District, The Contra Costa Food Bank, The Neighborhood Watch Protection Program, The Lindsey Wildlife Museum, and The Blackhawk Automobile Museum.

When Pete isn't busy with his real estate career, he enjoys hiking and fishing at his cabin in the Mount Lassen area and boating on Lake Almanor. He also likes to spend time touring Northern California on his motorcycle. Pete has two sons who currently attend Diablo Valley College in Pleasant Hill.

To Reach Pete Sabine
RE/MAX C.C. Connection
(925) 407-0606
Pete@ContraCostaLiving.com
ContraCostaLiving.com
or
see page 158

KEN DESHAIES is a real estate broker in Colorado. Ken is an Accredited Buyer Representative (ABR), Certified Residential Specialist (CRS), a graduate of the REALTOR® Institute (GRI), one of the first 500 Realtors® in the country to become a Certified Internet Real Estate Professional (e-PRO500), a Real Estate Cyberspace Specialist (RECS), an Allen F. Hainge CyberStar™ (an elite group of Realtors®

who have proven that they generate a significant portion of their business through the use of current technology), and is EcoBroker™ Certified. He has cauthored over 70 books on real estate. He was named CyberStar™ of the Year for 2002, and elected President of the Summit Association of REALTORS® for 2003. He served on the committee for the Colorado Association of REALTORS® that spearheaded the change in agency laws effective in 2003. Ken serves on the Grievance Committee of the Colorado Association of REALTORS® and is an iSucceed mentor.

Ken works in partnership with his wife, Mary, in their brokerage, SnowHome Properties. He began his real estate career in Denver in 1992 and has worked in Summit County since 1994. Located an hour west of Denver, Summit County is home to four ski resorts and the highest freshwater sailing lake in the United States. While selling resort real estate is similar in many ways to selling in a metropolitan area, it offers unique problems. For example, since two out of three buyers are buying nonresidential properties, marketed materials, use of the Internet and extensive use of digital photography are essential to a successful marketing plan.

Prior to real estate, Ken owned a private investigations firm for twelve years in Denver, employing and supervising as many as seven investigators and serving for a period as the President of the Professional Private Investigators Association of Colorado. In this work, he conducted numerous investigations into real estate transactions and fraud claims. Many of the stories in this book are based on Ken's experiences, both before and after he became a Realtor®. During much of this time, he was also a member of the Win/Win Business Forum of Denver and was its president for a year and a half.

To Reach Ken Deshaies
Ken@SnowHome.com
or see page 158

Section I

Selling Your Home: The Basics

1. Going It Alone

Before meeting you, we had bought a sign "For Sale by Owner" and wanted to sell our house by ourselves. After attending your seminar at Nolo Bookstore, Berkeley, we were convinced that an established marketing agent like your team would be the way to go. Your philosophy of revealing full documentation not only in presentation binder but also on the Internet is definitely a win/win approach for buyer and seller alike. Your timely guidance and professional advice, as the expert opinion of an author on real estate, is highly appreciated. We recommend your service to anyone who can use the help of an honest and experienced professional in real estate.

—Samuel and Mary Ho

Many people who are considering selling their home are not sure how to begin the process. Do you try to sell your house yourself, or do you enlist an agent? And if you do want to try to sell your house on your own, will word get out to that perfect buyer? The bottom line is that no matter which route you take to sell your home, you need to educate yourself as much as possible. Where the economic stakes can be high, knowledge is power. By reading about the following two experiences, you will see what can sometimes happen during the sale of a home and understand why it pays to be educated. Although the names have been changed, the following stories are real, and may help you to decide whether selling your house yourself will actually save you money.

A few years ago, Ken was searching for the right home for one of his buyers. He found a home not listed in the

Multiple Listing Service (the local Realtor® database in which all available properties for sale are listed) that was being sold by the owner (called a FSBO in Realtor® parlance). Since it appeared to fit his buyer's criteria, Ken called the number listed on the flyer that the owner had posted in his yard.

Most FSBOs understand that even though they want to save the listing commission, in almost 95 percent of the cases it will be a Realtor® who will bring in the buyer. So if they pay the Realtor® representing the buyer even something over half of a typical listing commission they still feel they are saving money by not having to pay commission to a listing agent as well. That was the case here, when John asked Ken to preview his home for his buyer. Later that day Ken visited with him and his wife, Lucille.

The home was in a family neighborhood, well maintained, and backed up to wetlands—things that would add value to the selling price as compared to other homes on the market. However, John and Lucille were planning a move to another town and had calculated into their asking price what they felt they would need to facilitate their move and the purchase of another home in their new location. While they did have some knowledge of other home sales in the neighborhood, their calculations led them to establish an asking price roughly 10 percent over those comparable sales. They were asking $690,000 for a home that would have been properly priced to sell at about $625,000. When Ken met with them he was prepared with a market analysis and tried to explain that the differential they were seeking was more than the market would bear. They encouraged Ken to bring them an offer but made it clear they would stick fairly close to their asking price.

Ken's buyers did look at the home but declined to make an offer. Most buyers will offer less than an asking price, but very few will offer when they feel there is too much difference between asking and market.

Ken watched as John's ads reflected a price reduction to $650,000, but nearly three months later he finally listed with a Realtor® at full commission. Unfortunately, now the asking price was back at $690,000 since the sellers were hoping to recover part of the Realtor® commission in the sale price. After three months of attempts to sell, the price had dropped twice to $665,000. It was clear the sellers were getting anxious to move. About that time, Ken showed the home to another buyer who liked it and made an offer. However, his clients were first time home buyers with little cash and they needed a little assistance to get into the property. Ken's offer was for $630,000 and he asked the sellers to carry a small note of $30,000 for five years. The buyers were creditworthy and otherwise fully capable of completing the purchase. However, Ken could not get the listing Realtor® to understand the simplicity of the financing and while the sellers would have taken the price, they declined the offer.

The home ultimately sold a couple of months later for $595,000–$95,000 less than their initial asking price, $35,000 less than Ken's buyer's offering price (the note would have been a bonus as it turned out), and around $20,000 to $30,000 less than the home would reasonably have sold for had it been properly listed from the start. Ken cannot tell you how many times he, and his Realtor® friends across the country have seen this very scenario— homes selling for less than market because they were priced too high and became "stale." Homes on the market for much longer than normal market conditions indicate often become the target of predatory buyers who understand that the seller is now more desperate and hence, willing to cut their price.

Although this story is not a guaranteed representation of the realities of selling your own home, what it does illustrate is that you must be educated. And often it pays to rely on an expert's education and experience. If you do decide that you are prepared for the task of selling your own home, here are some important suggestions:

1. Take the time to educate yourself about the process of real estate transactions. Know how the process works from beginning to end.

2. Know what activities, responsibilities and functions must be performed by outside professionals, such as inspectors, appraisers, lenders, or title officers.

3. Pay to have your house professionally appraised so that you price it correctly. If you are using this to determine pricing, a Realtor® will perform this function for you at no charge.

4. Have your home professionally inspected in advance so that you know what might need to be repaired. In some markets the sellers consider taking care of the items, but in the strong Bay Area sellers market, just about every home is sold "as is" with regard to whatever is revealed during inspections! Buyers will be told of the items but repairs are usually not made.

5. Establish a marketing budget and determine the best ways to allocate your expenses.

6. Look for a pre-approved rather than a pre-qualified buyer. There will be more on this distinction in the chapter regarding financing.

7. As a personal safety measure, *never* show your house alone.

8. And finally, understand that while it is your intention to save the real estate commission in the transaction, most buyers also understand

that and want the savings reflected in the purchase price.

Selling your house is not impossible, but it takes diligence, patience, diplomacy, and a willingness to set aside your own biases about your home so that other people's preferences can be understood and accommodated.

Knowing the Process

Before you decide to sell your own home, ask yourself the following essential questions to ensure that you are knowledgeable about these important aspects of real estate sales:

✓ Do I know how to properly value my home?

✓ Do I have a marketing strategy in order to reach the greatest number of potential buyers?

✓ Am I familiar with the Bay Area's legal requirements for purchase contracts and real estate transfers?

✓ Can I ensure that the buyer is financially able to purchase my home?

✓ Do I have the contacts needed to handle the closing transactions?

✓ Will my homeowner's insurance cover me for liability if a stranger, to whom I am showing my home, causes damage (to my home, my belongings, or me) or steals from me? (Recent stories involve people who steal prescription drugs from homes for their own use.)

✓ How are my negotiating skills?

✓ Am I prepared to give up a partial commission to an agent representing a buyer?

The bottom line is that you must make sure that you are prepared to deal with this major transaction. You should have a plan in place, and you should know who can help you with the aspects of the sale that you can't do alone. Just as money doesn't grow on trees, houses don't sell on their own. If you are selling your house yourself, you must be prepared to make a substantial investment of time. If you are not sure how to handle this intricate sales transaction, using a professional may save you a great deal of unnecessary complications and still net you more money at the end of the day. Then, if you really are prepared—no matter whether you have help or not—you should be able to successfully sell your home.

2. Using a Real Estate Agent

Pete kept me calm and optimistic. He explained the advantages and disadvantages of each offer clearly, guided me with his experience regarding financing and yet, never pushed me one way or another. Pete was especially good at follow-up and keeping me apprised of changes. I would recommend his services highly.

—Karin Sanford, Walnut Creek

A real estate agent and a Realtor® are not the same thing. Both may be experienced in the industry, but a Realtor® is a member of the National Association of REALTORS® and follows a specific code of ethics. (You will find more information on this in the following section, "Credentials.") Anyone who passes their state's real estate licensing exam can become an agent. They may also be referred to as a licensee or real estate salesperson in other parts of the book. There are no fee differences between hiring an agent and a Realtor®.

Although there are some costs associated with enlisting an agent or Realtor®, there are also substantial benefits. For instance, not only do Realtors® have access to thousands of potential buyers that a homeowner may not be aware of, they also have the knowledge to maximize financial and legal protection. Additionally, there is some element of chance involved in selling your home besides the obvious economic risk. Realtors® know important legal disclosure requirements. Agents are well aware of the fact that you are allowing complete strangers into your home, and therefore know what precautions you should take to protect both your family and your possessions. But these are just a few of the reasons why enlisting the help of a Realtor® is a good investment. A Realtor® can:

✓ Use extensive data and professional experience to assist in determining the best asking price for your home.

✓ Provide information about your home to thousands of potential buyers and their agents.

✓ Screen buyers and negotiate an offer as well as a purchase and sale agreement.

✓ Take on potential legal obligations and risks.

✓ Take you through every step of the process, all the way to closing.

What to Look For

Credentials

Picking an agent is a business decision that should be taken with the same deliberation as any other important financial decision. You will want an agent who specializes in your community, who is experienced, and who you are confident will work hard on your behalf. You've probably noticed that when we've used the term Realtor® in this book, it is capitalized and the registration mark is used. There is a reason for that. The term Realtor® is a trademark of the National Association of REALTORS® (NAR), and anyone who uses that term as part of their professional identity must be a member, not only of NAR but also of their state and local associations. Anyone who is not a member but is legitimately working in the real estate profession is still licensed by their state real estate commission and can be identified as an agent, a real estate salesperson, a real estate broker, and so on.

2. Using a Real Estate Agent

When you choose a Realtor®, however, it means that you have access to several things. NAR members have training available only to the Realtor® community. They have the benefit of local meetings and state and national conferences where they can network with other Realtors®. Many transactions are actually made for buyers and sellers at these events.

Members subscribe to a code of ethics, which commits them to conduct their business with a sense of fair play. The public has some recourse when they feel they have been lied to, mistreated, or cheated. They can file an ethics complaint with the local association requesting that a Realtor® be disciplined, or request arbitration if they feel they have actually been misrepresented. The Grievance Committee and the Professional Standards Committee of the organization handle these complaints. A member is always bound to submit to the grievance process when a complaint is initiated by a buyer or seller. It is a much simpler and less costly method of justice than going to court.

Members have to pay dues, and the Multiple Listing Service (MLS) charges other fees to maintain a membership in good standing, but the bottom line is that they are in a position to provide much better service to you than nonmembers.

Those who do not have the Realtor® designation operate independently. They often do not do enough business to justify the costs involved in belonging to the NAR. While not always the case, many are retired from other professions or are otherwise part-time in this profession, so they are not bound by the regulated code of ethics that governs a Realtor®'s actions, and in some areas they do not have the benefit of MLS access.

So for starters, get a Realtor®. You'll usually find the designation on their business card.

History

If you were taking in a roommate or boarder, you would screen that person to see if you were compatible. If you were renting out property, you would take a rental application and check out the renter's references and credit history. If you were going into business with or hiring someone, you would be smart to conduct a background check. It never hurts to know who you are working with. The same is true with a real estate agent. We need to prescreen, ask questions, get a feel for how compatible we might be and determine how well that professional can meet our particular needs.

If you have a friend in the business, it can be difficult to select someone else, but it might be the most valuable decision you can make. We have known people who listed their homes with friends who specialized in commercial sales but had never sold a house. You need to ask some questions before starting with any real estate agent. Don't sit down and say, "We're looking for a house in the $800,000 range." Try something like, "Before we start, I'd like to learn a few things about you." Interview your potential agent, ask questions, and determine the following important issues to your satisfaction.

Get a Full-Time Agent or a Professional Team

Most full-time agents work 50 to 60 hours a week or more. They are committed to their work and to their clients. A part-time agent is there to do business when it comes along, but either doesn't need the income a full time career produces, or isn't making it yet, and may hold two or more jobs. Within reasonable limits, a Realtor® should fit their schedule to yours, not the other way around, and should be available and easy to get in contact with regardless of their hours. On the other hand, agents who have spent some years building their business will often enlist assistants, or team members.

They may then be in a position to take more time off, but have qualified team members to show property and oversee the details of transactions. Team leaders train their team members in their system, and in the quality of customer service that the leader has developed over the years. Teams usually have specialists handling different parts of the transaction, so you will almost always have someone available to provide seamless service. This can be especially beneficial if your Realtor is on vacation or busy attending to other clients' needs.

Questions to ask:

✓ What other type of work do you do?

✓ Do you work full time in real estate?

✓ How flexible is your schedule?

✓ How available are you to show properties on weekdays, weekends, mornings, evenings?

Hire a Busy Agent

Ask your potential agent how many transaction sides they've completed last year and the year before. A *side* is one side of the sale. When one Realtor® has a listing and another one brings in the buyer, each produces one side. An agent who has closed only four to eight sides in a year is not doing enough business to merit having yours. And yet, the typical agent in the Bay Area only completes four transaction sides each year! Either they need money, just got started, or can't get enough business to survive and are on their way into another profession. An agent who has done four or eight sides is not making a great deal of money but is surviving and probably growing, and believe it or not, they're far above the national average.

An agent who is doing ten or more sides a year is very busy—usually for a reason. They have attracted business, hopefully because they have served people well, although some Realtors® generate a lot of business simply through smart advertising. It is, therefore, important to get a sense of how many transactions were results of referrals from past clients.

Questions to ask:

✓ How many sides did you close last year?

✓ Is that usual for you?

✓ How many sides did you close the year before?

Now that you know how busy the agent is, ask how many of those sides were a result of working with sellers and how many came from representing buyers.

Questions to ask:

✓ What percent of your business comes from representing sellers?

✓ How much of your business comes from referrals?

Check Out the Agent's Specialty

If you are selling a home, select an agent who specializes in residential sales. If you want to buy an apartment building or a business, select someone who specializes in commercial sales. There are numerous specialties in real estate, and your agent's specialty should be consistent with your goals. Note that in larger metropolitan areas, Realtors® also tend to specialize in geographic areas, in price ranges or with types of buyers. An agent who primarily sells million-dollar homes won't necessarily have the time for a $500,000 home.

Questions to ask:

✓ Do you have a specialty?

✓ What are the price ranges of the homes you market?

✓ What area/region do you specialize in?

✓ Do you sell commercial and residential real estate?

Make Sure the Agent Is Technologically Current

In today's world, it is vitally important to work with professionals who are computer literate and understand the latest gadgets designed to improve service to their customers. What does that mean?

First, many states require Realtors® to use certain forms in real estate transactions. In California, most good agents are using software computer programs, which presents the quickest most accurate way to generate contracts or offers to purchase. Those who continue to write their contracts by hand or use a typewriter in order to fill in the blanks on standard forms are living in the past as well as demonstrating an unwillingness to keep up with the times. They may not be capable of providing the best service.

Other types of software allow Realtors® to track their customers' needs, access increasingly sophisticated MLS systems and communicate via email. Digital cameras allow photos and virtual tours of your home complete with interior and exterior views.

If the real estate agent you are interviewing is not able to utilize a computer, beat a hasty retreat. Make sure when an agent says they're computerized, they don't just rely on an assistant or a shared secretary to do all the computer work for them. Your house should have as much Internet exposure as possible. Your wonderful home could be passed over while a competing house that is visible on the Internet is quickly snatched up.

Questions to ask:

✓ Can I have your email address?

✓ What is the address of your website? Do you have more than one? What others do you link to? What sites link to yours?

✓ What systems do you have in place to follow up on your Internet leads?

✓ Will you take digital pictures of my home? How many pictures will appear in the MLS and in other marketing materials? Will you create a virtual tour of my home?

✓ Do you also do print advertising?

✓ Can you show me samples of your listings, flyers, and websites?

✓ What is your marketing plan—What are the ways in which you generate leads?

✓ What other technology do you employ in your business?

Training

Anyone worth their salt in any profession continues to update their knowledge about the work they do. Doctors, lawyers, and mechanics face an ever-changing world when it comes to their professions and must take classes in order to continue to be of service to their customers. The same is true of Realtors®.

California state law requires continuing education, but the requirements are usually minimal: 45 hours every four years for individuals holding a license. Good Realtors® find the time to take much more training than that. There are a number of designations denoting certain continuing education landmarks, which are often signified on business cards as acronyms following the name. While some may be in areas not related to residential sales, all show a commitment on behalf of the Realtor® to keep their professional skills honed, and that's good. Do not work with someone who demonstrates no interest in continuing education. Look for some of the following designations on your prospective agent's business card:

GRI—Graduate, Realtor® Institute—represents approximately 90 hours of advanced education beyond the training that is required to be licensed. It is usually the first step toward becoming more informed and professional.

CRS—Certified Residential Specialist—requires completion of numerous two- to three-day classes held around the country. It takes the average Realtor® a few years to complete and usually costs $5,000 to $10,000 in tuition and travel costs. It provides significantly increased and detailed knowledge in residential issues and is the "graduate degree" of residential sales. Graduates are members of the Residential Sales Council (RSC) and receive continuing information in a variety of ways to keep them abreast of new issues in the area.

e-PRO—Certified Internet Real Estate Professional— this is the only certification program of its kind recognized nationwide and endorsed by the National Association of REALTORS®. Those searching for a Realtor® can have confidence that e-PRO graduates are Internet savvy. They not only take Internet-empowered consumers seriously, but are able to meet their online needs as well.

ABR—Accredited Buyer Representative: Those with an ABR designation have completed additional training with the intent of learning new negotiating tactics and skills. Additionally, Accredited Buyer Representatives must maintain membership in the Real Estate Buyer Agency Council (REBAC) where they are kept continuously updated and informed about how to represent buyers.

SRES—Seniors Real Estate Specialist: Those holding this designation are Realtors® who are qualified to meet the special needs and concerns of maturing Americans. A national program since 1998, The Senior Advantage Real Estate Council® (SAREC®) offers a specific designation, SRES, to identify those members who have successfully completed its education program along with other prerequisites. By earning the SRES designation, your Realtor® has demonstrated requisite knowledge and expertise to counsel senior clients through major financial and life-style transitions involved in relocating, refinancing, or selling the family home.

CyberStar—An Allen F. Hainge CyberStar is one of an elite group of Realtors® from around the country and abroad (membership by invitation only) who have proven efficiency in the use of technology and have agreed to serve as teaching professionals with Allen. They work well with people on the Internet, via email and yes, in person. They are top producers in their markets, and they have exclusive territories. Their websites are often the most innovative and provide the most local information.

Attitude

We just cannot end this section without a discussion concerning attitude and disposition. A good, winning attitude makes up for a lot. We'd much rather work with a newly licensed agent who really wants to help than some old curmudgeon who has been in the profession for years, thinks they have all the answers, and won't listen to anything new. There are a lot of worn-out real estate agents who have "seen it all" still occupying desk space in offices across the country.

Your initial interview with a prospective agent will tell you a lot about their approach to life. Work with an optimist, not a pessimist. Listen to their answers to your questions. Are they saying, "Your house is going to be hard to sell," or "It might be difficult to find the right buyer, but I know that the right exposure can get your house sold."

Look for a good, positive attitude as part of your evaluation process.

Summary and Final Questions

Your success in selling your home is dependent on the quality of the agent you select to represent you in that sale. You know that an agent doesn't get paid until a sale occurs. So, would you be concerned if an agent were unable or afraid to spend the necessary money to properly expose your home to potential buyers? Would you be concerned if an agent simply put your property listing into our multiple listing service (MLS), put up a sign and prayed that it would sell?

In the Bay Area, there are thousands of Realtors®, but 20 percent of the agents handle the majority of the the real estate transactions. You would be well advised to determine where your agent ranks. This is an important decision. So, here are our recommendations.

Choose an agent who:

✓ Knows how to get your home the best exposure. More exposure increases the chances of your home selling for the best price.

✓ Has a personal website and that the site is content-rich and places well in the Internet search engines. In 2005, 80 percent of all homebuyers in the United States started on the Internet. Often, they selected their agent prior to shopping for their home.

✓ Advertises in print publications. Though not the best way to obtain buyers, repetition of the company name will create more traffic for all.

✓ Spends an appropriate amount of money on other advertising.

✓ Produces a virtual tour or slide show of your property and places it on the Internet for buyers to see. Two-thirds of buyers who viewed properties on the Internet indicated that they look for virtual tours, and all website visitors want to see lots of photos.

✓ Knows how to use a camera and uses it frequently. Too many agents take only one photo of a property and some take none at all. Digital cameras make taking photos easy and inexpensive. There is no reason that you should not have the maximum number of photos allowed in your MLS listing and many more on agent and other websites. The only exception might be if you were selling a distressed property that just did not photograph well at all— and even then photos would be a great help to excite the people who really want a major fixer!

✓ Believes in continuing education to keep up on the latest in selling techniques, and to network with agents locally and in other locales. Most successful agents attend conferences around the country where they meet other agents, and they then refer business to each other.

✓ Covers their market. If a successful agent works well in the entire geographic market serviced by the local MLS, it is better to work with that agent than one who is less successful, but closer to your home.

While no one can guarantee a quick sale, an agent who performs with the above qualifications will make your selling experience smoother, will cause you less anxiety, and will provide the highest possibility for a successful sale.

Agency—Liability

So that you can understand how representation works, it is important to discuss the concept of agency. It's easy to bandy about words like *seller's agency* and *real estate agency*, but the fact of the matter is that *agency* is a legal term. Its use confers a legal obligation and some legal liability.

Let's say, for example, your parents are going to be away on vacation for an extended period of time. While they are gone, they want someone to deposit their checks, pay their bills, and carry on business for them as usual. What they want, in fact, is someone to keep their best interests in mind and to act accordingly. They ask you to represent them, to handle the paperwork in their absence. In order for you to legally perform those functions on their behalf, they would have to sign a document giving you power to act for them in those matters. This document is called a *power of attorney*, and it makes you their legal representative. The person giving the power is known as the *principal,* while the individual who has been given the power is known as the *agent.*

If you were to call your parents' banker in their absence and ask to transfer money from one account to another, the banker would refuse—unless you can prove you are the agent of your parents. In order to do that, you would have to provide their banker with a copy of the power of attorney.

It is also important to understand that a person empowered to be an agent may be in a better position to handle the principal's business than is the principal. The agent is either physically in a better location to handle business for the principal, or is more knowledgeable about the matters to be handled than the principal.

Vicarious Liability

An important aspect of agency to be familiar with is *vicarious liability.* Most people understand that a liability is a risk; it's an exposure. You take on the possibility of a liability when you hire or authorize a person to take actions on your behalf. You are still liable (pursuant to a specific power of attorney for the transaction at hand) for that individual's actions. Your child could damage the property of another, and you might be held responsible for reparations. That is *vicarious liability.* It is extending your risk through reliance on, or responsibility for, others.

In real estate transactions, every time you engage a real estate agent to represent you, you take on some vicarious liability if they act negligibly or unethically on your behalf within the scope of their authority. You rely on your agent to analyze a situation, make and give expert advice and make recommendations on your behalf that are in your best interest. You have also engaged that agent because you believe their knowledge in this area is greater than yours.

When you engage a Realtor® to represent you, it will behoove you to ensure your agent is experienced, knowledgeable, professional, and willing and able to work for you. California state law requires real estate licensees who are acting as agents of sellers or buyers of property to advise the potential sellers or buyers with whom they work of the nature of their agency relationship, and the rights and obligations it creates.

Understanding Agency Relationships and Disclosure Laws

Seller's Agency

When you list your home for sale, you employ a seller's agent to represent you in the transaction. A seller's agent has, without limitation, the following fiduciary duties to the seller: to employ the utmost care, integrity, honesty, and loyalty in dealings with the client.

The obligations of a seller's agent are also subject to any specific provisions set forth in a listing agreement between the agent and the seller. In dealings with the buyer, a seller's agent should (a) diligently exercise reasonable skill and care in performance of the agent's duties; (b) transact business honestly, fairly and in good faith; and (c) disclose all facts known to the agent materially affecting the value or desirability of the property, except as otherwise provided by law.

Buyer's Agency

If you are buying a home, you can work with an agent as a buyer's agent. A buyer agency relationship exists when the agent represents the buyer exclusively in the real estate transaction. The agent works on behalf of, and in the best interest of, the buyer. The source of the agent's compensation does not determine the agency relationship with the client.

If you are a buyer and choose to work with a buyer's agent, you may be asked to sign a buyer-broker agreement that must outline the duties of both the buyer and the agent, the duration of contract, any fees (what fees will be earned, who pays and when), and any other duties required by both parties.

A buyer's agent has, without limitation, the following fiduciary duties to the buyer: to employ the utmost care, integrity, honesty, and loyalty in dealings with the client. The obligations of a buyer's agent are also subject to any specific provisions set forth in an agreement between the agent and the buyer, including, as with a seller's agent, a disclosure of all facts known to the agent that may affect the value or desirability of the property.

In dealing with the seller, a buyer's agent should (a) exercise reasonable skill and care in performance of the agent's duties; (b) transact business honestly, fairly and in good faith; and (c) disclose all the facts known to the agent materially affecting the buyer's ability and/or willingness to perform a contract to acquire a seller's property that are not inconsistent with the agent's fiduciary duties to the buyer, including confidentiality.

While buyer's agency seems clear cut, and usually is, problems can sometimes arise. That's why we use forms prepared by the California Association of Realtors® (CAR) and make disclosures in writing. For example, in Silicon Valley, an issue arose that involved the same real estate company, with multiple offices under the same ownership, representing multiple buyers who made offers on the same property. A case arose in which a buyer became very angry that the same brokerage represented 4 out of 20 potential buyers for a property on which he was bidding, and filed a lawsuit. Of course, with multiple offers, we never know the details, or who has the other offers, but most buyers don't understand this. So, now, in order to make everything clear for our clients, we use a consent form to disclose that we may represent more than one buyer or seller.

Dual Agency

This is not a new term, but its use poses a hurdle many feel is impossible to overcome. Dual agency exists whenever the same real estate broker represents both the buyer and seller. When you sign a listing or buyer agreement with an agent, you are actually retaining the agent's entire brokerage to represent you in your purchase or sale. Dual agency requires the broker to simultaneously be an agent and advocate for both the buyer and seller in the same transaction. Obviously, this can create conflicting allegiances.

For instance, one real estate broker might supervise five different offices with the same franchise, so any two real estate agents working in one of those offices would have a dual agency situation if one represents the buyer and the other represents the seller. If the other agent is with the same franchise, but not one of the five offices supervised by the same broker, there is *no* dual agency. When an agent with one brokerage represents a seller, and an agent in another brokerage represents a buyer, there is little potential for conflict of interest.

In theory, a dual agent owes both the buyer and seller the same fiduciary duties as if the agent represented each alone. These duties include loyalty, disclosure, confidentiality, reasonable care, and diligence. By consenting to dual agency, the conflicting duties to buyer and seller are reconciled and instead the dual agent is required to act with equality and fairness to each party. In addition, most of the other fiduciary obligations are affected because of the contrasting motivations of buyer and seller, who have agreed that the consensual dual agency will not favor the interests of one over those of another.

In a dual agency relationship, your agent cannot give uneven loyalty to either side. The agent must simply present the facts and information within their knowledge and insist the buyer and seller make their own decisions, without influence from an agent. The agent may not, without express written permission of one party, disclose the bottom line to the other party, and vice versa. This protects the negotiating edge that each party has.

There Are Advantages to Dual Agency

As much as some may feel dual agency can be harmful to consumers, it does have some advantages. If you are dealing with only one firm, and especially if there is only one individual agent involved, your lines of communication are shorter. For example, if you ask your agent a question that requires input from the other party, you are likely to get a faster answer, as there is one less individual in the chain of communication.

To protect yourself, discuss the firm's agency policy in your initial contact with them, and ask them to explain how and if they deal with dual agency. Of course, the agent you choose will also have to be experienced and competent in the rest of the skills needed to serve you, which we will address in other areas of this book. A real estate firm can legally be a dual agent only with the knowledge and written consent of both the buyer and seller.

Non-Agency

Some states have embraced an alternative to dual agency: non-agency. In a non-agency relationship, the firm has no fiduciary responsibilities to either party. This arrangement is unattractive to consumers for the obvious reason: There are very few circumstances in which you would hire a firm that has no responsibility to you, and possibly no liability if they damage you. We recommend you strongly consider your options as non-agency affords you the least amount of representation.

Non-Exclusive Agency

In California we have something called non-exclusive agency. In non-exclusive agency, an agent basically just takes the seller's listing, puts it in the MLS and waits for a buyer. The agent will not spend time marketing the home or giving the seller advice. This type of relationship is often used in the flat-fee, or fee-for service brokerages.

Disclosure

In the past, it was up to the seller to inquire about the types of relationships they could have with a broker and what each meant. Most states recognized that this was impractical. How could an unsophisticated consumer be knowledgeable in real estate agency when even most brokers were not? A majority of states eventually shifted the obligation of disclosure to the broker. Presently, the law requires an agent to inform their seller or buyer about the different agency relationships upon the first substantive contact.

You must be an educated consumer. When interviewing potential Realtors® to represent you as either a seller's or buyer's agent, if that Realtor® fails to discuss the various choices set forth above, you may wish to reconsider your decision to employ that individual. The agent may be unaware of the law, or is intentionally not informing you of your choices. In either case, they may be doing you a disservice.

Types of Listing Agreements

If you are seeking an agent to help you in the process of selling your home, there are several routes that you can take depending upon the kind of service that you want. Whether you just need minimal services or want exclusive representation by a real estate agent to sell your home, you will most likely sign some kind of listing agreement. Face it, real estate agents have access to buyers and can sell your home much more quickly by pooling all their resources than you can with just a "For Sale" sign on your front lawn. Below are some of your options when signing a listing agreement, ranging from the *exclusive right to sell* to a *one-time show*.

Exclusive Right to Sell

If you are looking for the best representation and the widest market exposure through which to sell (remember, the more potential buyers who see your home, the better your offer will be), an exclusive right to sell agreement with an agent you trust is the best option you have. With this kind of agreement, you work with one listing agent who will market your home through every channel. They will place your home in the Multiple Listing Service (MLS), market your home to the public and to other agents representing buyers, and possibly hold open houses to find potential buyers.

With this kind of listing agreement, you will get the full array of services from your Realtor®, while your Realtor® is guaranteed a commission when your home sells regardless of who brings in the buyer. However, this does not mean that your agent will be the only agent involved in the transaction. While an agent can certainly bring in one of their own buyers, an agent's most powerful marketing tool is networking with a whole array of agents who are representing clients interested in buying your home. This kind of arrangement can get your house the most exposure and hopefully an offer with the best price and terms, and you'll end up with the best deal.

An exclusive right to sell agreement is the most common type of listing because of the services it provides and because the agent is guaranteed a commission when your house sells. Therefore, the agent will be appropriately compensated for the amount of time, money and expertise that goes into the sale of your home.

Open Listing

If you are selling your house on your own but are still willing to work with an agent to bring in a buyer, an open listing is what is most commonly used. In an open listing, a real estate agent representing a buyer has the ability to show your home to their client if it suits the client's needs. If their client buys the home, the agent earns a commission.

There is nothing exclusive about this type of agreement and a seller can offer such listings to any agent who is interested. The only reason that an agent would show your home is because they have a particular buyer in mind who's criteria is a convenient match for your home. Therefore, in an open listing, no agent will bother to market your home or place it in the MLS because they will only earn a commission through a buyer that they bring in.

One-Time Show

A one-time show listing is similar to an open listing. With a one-time show listing, the seller is not represented by an agent but allows an agent to bring in one of their buyers and receive a commission. If you are selling your home on your own, and an agent brings in one of their clients, they might ask you to sign a one-time show listing. In this case, the agent bringing in the buyer is guaranteed a commission should their buyer purchase your home.

Like an open listing, your home won't be marketed or placed on the MLS. You will simply have to wait until an agent has a buyer who is interested in your home. Another option is to sign a commission or single party compensation agreement that obligates the seller to compensate an agent only if their buyer makes an acceptable purchase offer and escrow closes successfully.

Exclusive Agency Listing

An exclusive agency listing is similar to an exclusive right to sell except the agent listing your home is not guaranteed a commission. For this reason, there are very few agents who will sign this type of listing agreement and, in the end, both you and your agent can end up losing. In an exclusive agency listing, an agent is allowed to list and market your home and will get a commission if they sell your home through any real estate agent or company. However, the seller is also able to find their own buyer, and if they do, the agent does not get any commission despite the fact that they put work into marketing your home. For this reason, many agents who sign an exclusive agency listing will not market your home because they are not guaranteed a commission for time and money spent. Most likely, an agent will just place your home in the MLS and see what happens.

Commissions

Commissions in this country have historically been paid out of the proceeds of the sale, so it has been presumed that the seller actually pays the commissions; however, this is not entirely true. Some professionals believe that because it is the buyer who actually brings the money to the transaction, the buyer pays the commission.

In addition, new agency laws have started to change this tradition by stating that any party to a transaction may pay any broker's compensation, without creating or terminating any agency relationship within that transaction. And more importantly, home values in this country are established with real estate commissions factored in because home sales have been, and almost always are, handled by real estate agents. The cost of that handling becomes part of the ultimate sale price and value of the home. Therefore, it becomes a moot point who pays the commission—it is simply part of the home value, paid out of the proceeds of the sale. Be aware that listing commission amounts or percentages are negotiable, and the form of commission agreed to may vary as well. There is no "standard" or "normal" commission.

Another thing to be aware of is that agents are not allowed to charge you any fee on top of their commission unless it is explicitly stated in writing.

Just as in many complex transactions, expertise costs money, but it is usually well worth the investment. A seller should focus on the amount of net sales proceeds after all costs are paid. Commissions play an important role in getting top dollar for your home. When you offer the buyer's agent a competitive commission, it increases your odds for full exposure and showing activity to all qualified buyers in your area. What matters most is not how much you pay, but how much you net at close of escrow.

Some sellers focus only on cost, and believe that they're better off by paying a lower commission. They can only reduce their sales costs to zero...if both they and the buyers are unrepresented. In fact, what matters most is the size of the sales proceeds check at closing. The best way to increase *that* is by selling your home for the highest possible price!

Ira knows that each incremental offer he generates for the seller raises the final selling price by 2.5–4.0 percent. In other words, when he generates four offers for the seller, his listings sell for 10–16 percent above the asking price! One listing actually received 14 offers and sold for 43 percent above the asking price! Commission plays an important role in selling for excellent prices—when you offer the buyer's agent a fair commission, they go out of their way to show their clients your home rather than a different home. We've found that it's always best for sellers to pay a fair commission. What matters most is not how much you pay, but what you net!

How Much Goes to Your Agent?

The listing agent offers half their listing commission to an agent working with a buyer who brings in a successful contract, so it is unusual for the listing agent to keep the entire listing commission. Each of those agents then has to split their portion of the commission with their broker. The broker usually incurs the cost of keeping an office open, keeping it staffed and equipped, and the broker's portion of the listing agent's split is meant to pay for that overhead and, hopefully, provide some profit. If your agent is the broker, then they are incurring those costs themselves.

Studies have shown that the cost of being in business in real estate can amount to much more than 50 percent of earnings. Now, obviously, a broker whose agents sell less will have a higher percentage of earnings going to overhead, and one who sells more can expect less overhead and more profit. It is not unusual for half the agent's split to go to the broker. Many times, that split is structured more in favor of the agent as the agent's production goes up. Your listing agent may only be keeping one-quarter of the listing commission that you are paying—and your agent has additional expenses of their own. Brokers do not cover all costs. Agents generally have to provide their own vehicles for showing (and they cannot be old and run down), their own cell phones, pay their own dues, insurance, continuing education and at least part of their advertising costs.

How important is the sale of your home at the best price and in a timely manner? As with any professional service, you can search for the least expensive vendor or you can search for the most qualified. The most qualified will generally cost you more, but you can often measure the savings. At the very least, you get the additional peace of mind when knowing you're in good hands.

Limited Service Brokers

Usually, they are often the brokers who provide "discount services" and who don't spend as much money and effort getting exposure for your property. But they are also the brokers who *advertise* that they will charge you less than anyone else. There are often a couple of problems associated with such listings. Once the property has been on the market too long without a sale, even if it has been priced properly, it may have to come down in price in order to generate new interest. There are companies now that will take your property listing and not provide *any* service—with the exception of placing the property in the local MLS for an additional fee. Agents working with buyers are not offered a cooperative selling commission, or if they are, it's a nominal fee. So, the agent is instructed to negotiate the buyer's offer directly with the seller. The buyer's agent, to get paid for their work, will have to collect their commission directly from the buyer. And if the agent doubts their ability to get paid if they sell your property, what do you think are the prospects of them actually showing it?

Now, consider if you were the buyer and had to pay your agent's commission on top of paying for the home. You could not include the commission in the financing, because it is not in the purchase price. So, it would be additional money out of pocket.

If financing were to be part of the transaction, you would likely lose that buyer. And if you will be paying the buyer's agent directly, you might as well engage a full service Realtor® from the beginning, eliminate the headaches and have someone capable, willing and obligated to provide you with good advice throughout the listing sale process.

Included in the mix are those entities called "bundled service" companies. These are companies that may provide the entire range of real estate service, but let you choose which you want. You may decide, for example, to hold your own open house and do your own advertising, and hence, pay a smaller fee.

Ultimately, you get to decide full-service or less. Just be aware of the differences. Accepting less service may save you money, but it places added burden on you to help create a sale.

As of this writing, two states have passed legislation requiring licensed real estate agents to provide a set minimum amount of service, regardless of what they charge. And a number of additional states are considering similar legislation. Part of the impetus has been complaints from homeowners who did not understand that they would have to do virtually everything in the transaction, and pay the fees, as well.

3. The Role of the Internet

Samia helped us sell the house, in a terribly slow market, in three short weeks! She helped us price the house correctly which was a big factor in selling the house quickly. Samia also has an eye for detail and her organized nature makes her a wonderful Realtor® to have. She gave us a lot of help in getting the house on the market. I would recommend anyone buying or selling a house to go to Samia.

—Saloni Sarin, Sun Microsystems

Mollie Wasserman's Real Estate Internet Warning©

Despite advertising claims to the contrary, the Internet is not an experienced real estate professional. It cannot consult, counsel, advise, have knowledge of local laws and market conditions, make judgments, "own" the result or, most importantly, understand your individual goals and needs and care about you as a client. Furthermore, data by itself can be very misleading. To obtain an accurate interpretation of any information you're receiving online, please contact your Realtor®.

—Mollie Wasserman

Given the revolution in technology that we've experienced over the last few years we must look at *what technology can and cannot do.*

Now let's be clear: Technology, and specifically the Internet, is a wonderful thing! Technology is a fabulous way to gather data and it can do *functionary* tasks better, faster and cheaper than any human being ever could. But the danger does not lie in understanding that technology. The danger is that by itself, the Internet can never provide the *fiduciary* counsel required for services such as lending, law, and real estate.

Functionary, fiduciary—why do we keep using these words? It's very important to understand the difference between the data that you can get online, and the advice, counsel, and interpretation of that data that only your Realtor® can provide if you're to get the best advice and service when you sell a home.

Information Versus Knowledge

As Internet-savvy Realtors® who generate a significant portion of our business online, we are big believers in the free flow of information. You will find that both online and off, the new breed of Realtor® usually provides the most complete sources of information you'll find anywhere.

Yet, we have had many of our colleagues question why we give out so much information, often saying: "If you give out too much information, people will have no reason to call you." We disagree. Although we provide information freely, we have never have a shortage of requests to retain our services. That's because there's a big difference between *information* and *knowledge*.

John Tuccillo states in his book, *The Eight New Rules of Real Estate*, "Information is a collection of facts or observations about reality. Knowledge is actionable." In today's information age, consumers can increasingly get all the information that they want or need, but it's useless unless someone with expertise in the field can provide the knowledge to allow them to correctly act on it. *Information, without the context of a pro who can share the day-to-day knowledge of the industry, is just* data. *If a consumer were to act on it without context, they could very well reach incorrect conclusions and achieve undesirable results.*

Information is like sand on a beach—it's plentiful and anyone can find it. But if you want to build a sandcastle, you may want to consult the Sandmaster who lives on the beach to tell you how much water to use, where to build, what weather conditions are best for building, and most importantly, when the tide comes in and how far up. Without this knowledge, you could spend an entire afternoon having your work prematurely washed away long before you completed your masterpiece.

Myths Involving Real Estate and the Internet

People love to surf the web when it comes to real estate. It's estimated that last year, over 80 percent of homebuyers started their searches online. But there are myths about what the Internet can and cannot do. The following myth is one of our favorites:

"The Internet is great! I can . . .

(1) buy a book

(2) buy an airline ticket

(3) buy or sell a house

(4) get legal advice

(5) receive a medical opinion
    . . . *all* online!"

At what point did the above statement step over the line from fact to myth? If you say after number two, the airline ticket, give yourself a gold star! What's the difference between the first two products and the last three services? Simple. *The first two are commodities bought mostly by price, the last three are services that require counsel, advice, knowledge, and understanding of your individual needs.* The first two are functionary products, the last three are fiduciary services. You can purchase the first two products entirely online and probably save money in the process. In regards to the last three services, the Internet is a great place to start your search for service providers. But if you try to "go it alone" with just the data you find online, you will very likely put your personal health or wealth at risk if you don't consult a local provider who understands your individual needs and is accountable for their services.

Let's look at an obvious example before turning to real estate. Let's say there's an online site called WeKnowLaws-r-us.com. For $39.95, payable in advance by credit card, you can receive a "legal opinion." Does this opinion come from an attorney, a paralegal or a truck driver? The site *says* it's from an attorney, but how do you know for sure? And what if you take this legal advice and your case turns out badly? How do you get out of the deeper legal dilemma you're now in? There is no due diligence online. Local attorneys who are dependent on referrals for future business have a great incentive to stand behind their advice and counsel. Does whoever at WeKnowLaw out there in Dot-Com Land care if you're unhappy with their opinion? In other words, what happens if something goes wrong?

There are online lenders companies that advertise everywhere, but we don't recommend them for a few reasons. First, much of the loan process still has to be done locally, so there's little economy to doing the process online, and more importantly, many consumers are finally catching on that interest rates and financing programs are very vulnerable to the old bait and switch. Do you really think for a moment that the online loan company in Anywhere Land is particularly concerned if you're unhappy with their services? Second, agents like dealing with local lenders—it pays to have a preapproval letter from a local lender. Local lenders derive business from local Realtors® and the community. Therefore, they have to make the situation right because they must be *accountable*! The national dot-com isn't. Now, as we said earlier, the Internet is a wonderful place to shop rates and programs as well as to educate yourself on the loan process. But afterwards, do yourself a favor and bring the best package to your Realtor's® recommended lender and ask if they can match it. Either they will, or they'll tell you why they can't. You can get your loan anywhere, but it's best to make sure you are pre-approved with a good local lender.

Have you ever been to a medical website? There are many wonderful sites out there. If you were to go to one to become a more educated patient, and then take your questions and concerns to your doctor, that would be a very smart use of the Internet. If, however, you were to go to a site and attempt to diagnose yourself, that would be a very unintelligent use of information, with potentially disastrous results.

Real estate is an interesting field in that it combines functionary tasks with fiduciary counsel. Functionary tasks such as property searches or accessing home sales data can always be done cheaper, faster, and better by technology. If that was the whole of real estate, we'd be the first to applaud the national dot-coms popping up online promising to provide you these services without your having to leave the computer. But the problem is, these companies don't tell you what you *don't* get. As an example, there are a couple of companies that heavily advertise a *free* home valuation online. All you have to do is give them a street address and it's yours. So what *do* you get? (Drum roll please.) A list of homes sold within a one-mile radius of that address. For instance, Elmwood/ Claremont, one of Berkeley's nicest neighborhoods, has Ashby Avenue, a well-traveled street with a state highway running through it. This "home valuation" company would just mention a major highway as a negative. But Ashby is really just a busy street, and not what someone would perceive as a highway. Go one block off Ashby and you'll find grand, spacious homes on tree lined streets! The online market analysis won't know how the inside of the home compares with others. What about sewer abatements or the newest regulations? A national dot-com can't advise you of any of those things, which could greatly affect the value of the property; but a Realtor® who's working in your interest can.

Please remember that while the Internet can provide information, it cannot interpret it! A Realtor®'s real value is not just in using technology to market your home, it is also in bringing those buyers to you, and helping you to make the most money when selling your home!

4. How Much Is Your Home Really Worth?

Personalized service and attention to detail were important to me. Pete and his team exceeded my expectations. He made sure that I looked at things from different perspectives to understand the ramifications of each decision.

—Brian Dulac, Walnut Creek

When you are ready to sell your home, you must determine the "asking" price with your Realtor®'s advice. We've found that the wisest sellers put their home on the market at a "strategic price"—the price at which it will sell with several offers. When our marketing generates multiple offers, the home sells for more than asking price, and with fewer contingencies in the buyers' offers. The other advantage of having multiple offers is that you can usually put one of them into "backup" position, so that if the person whose offer you accepted becomes unreasonable, you have the option of going to the "understudy." The strategic price is a price at the lower end of the "range" of sales prices, but one which would be acceptable to you if it was the only offer. We feel strongly that a seller should not put their home on the market at a price which they would not be willing to accept.

One important component to "strategic pricing" is that you should set a date, usually 7 to 10 days after the home comes on the market, that you will be reviewing offers. If you accept an offer right after the home comes on the market, you very likely will sell for less than you could have otherwise received!

Here is another reason to hire a Realtor®. A good, experienced Realtor® in your area will often know just by looking at your home what it can expect to sell for in the current market. Not only might they know the sale prices of similar homes that have sold in the neighborhood, but your Realtor® may know the homes' original listing prices and how much sellers in your neighborhood have been willing to negotiate.

Whether or not you decide to use a Realtor®, there are two predominant ways to determine a home's value: an appraisal and a comparative market analysis. What you should expect to learn through either process is the approximate value of your home. The reality is that until your home actually sells, there is no precise way to determine exactly what your home is worth. In the business, we say that your home is worth exactly what someone pays for it. An appraiser will tell you that a home's value is equal to an amount agreed to between an able and willing buyer and an able and willing seller, when neither person is unduly influenced by outside forces.

Home Appraisal

An appraisal is usually ordered by the buyer's lender after an offer has been accepted. We don't recommend that the seller obtain an appraisal to determine market value. The best way is for you and your Realtor® to review recent comparable sales, and the current "temperature" of the market, and price strategically.

Market Value

The most common method used by Realtors® to determine the sales price of your home is a *comparative market analysis* (CMA). A CMA is an estimated value of your home, based on the sales price and similar attributes of other properties in the area. A CMA may be less precise than an appraisal, but it is really the best method in determining the asking price of your home.

It will also help if, with your Realtor®, you look at other comparable homes currently on the market in your area and compare their similarities and differences. This will help you decide the list price of your home, and help you see exactly who you may be competing against for that perfect buyer.

Remember that regardless of what list price you choose, the actual sales price may be slightly higher or lower. If for some reason your house is not selling, you and your Realtor® should consider lowering the price. Beware of having your mind set on some magic number given by a CMA or based on your *need* alone. Remember that these are only approximations of the real value of your home. The economy and the market can actually change in relatively short periods of time. In addition, no matter how you try to determine a price, your home may have peculiarities that are just not present in any other home.

5. Selling Your Home in an Up or Down Market

Please allow us to express our heartfelt thank you to Carol and Ira for their wonderful job obtaining an astounding offer toward the sale of our home in Rockridge (Oakland, California) recently. Working with you two presents a unique opportunity for home buyers/sellers. One that can best be described through the old cliché of "two for the price of one." The combination of Ira's masterful, Internet/tech-savvy marketing and Carol's astute analysis and detailed administration of the entire sales process produced results exceeding our highest expectation. Again, thanks so much for a job well done, and best wishes toward all future endeavors!

—Todd and Mary Ryder

Although the asking price may need slight modifications, regardless of the market, a good Realtor® will be able to help you sell your home. This may be important to the many sellers out there who cannot wait for a market turnaround to sell. The reality is that if it is priced competitively and in a condition that appeals to the average buyer, you should be able to sell your home regardless of the market if the house is priced competively/strategically.

Besides the "asking" price, there are many things that can affect how quickly you sell your home, but we will start with price.

Price

For obvious reasons, the asking price is the most important factor in determining how quickly your home will sell. Despite the desire to make sure that you price your home high enough to make a profit, and leave room to negotiate, you should be aware that overpricing your home is the most common, serious, correctable, and dangerous mistake that you can make as a seller.

A home may be overpriced for many reasons. Some sellers consider their first asking price to be a "trial balloon," where they just want to see if they can attract a better-than-normal offer. Others simply insist that their home is worth more than any objective market analysis would indicate. For example, sellers who have been trying to sell their house themselves for months may now want to raise the price since they are paying a Realtor® for representation; the sellers still want their net price, so they try to add sales commissions to the listed price. Homes like this usually stay on the market the longest and end up being sold for less than market value. One of the primary reasons so many FSBOs fail is because the seller is personally biased. It is easy to convince yourself that something you own is worth more than its real value. It's also why so many Realtors®, when selling their own homes, actually list with other Realtors®, or at least rely on the advice of others. Objectivity is paramount.

Price and Timing are Everything

Well-priced homes can, and often do, sell quickly—an infinitely more convenient situation for any seller and their family!

Remember, there are almost always a number of prospects waiting for your listing—people who have looked in your price range and neighborhood but not found the right property—and want to see everything new when it comes on the market. Once the buyers already in the market have visited, you can typically expect showings to drop to a more regular level, usually after two weeks.

Selling Price Vs. Timing

A few years ago, Ken's son and daughter-in-law asked him to help them sell their home. Since they were in another community, he referred them to a trusted Realtor® friend who knew their neighborhood well. The evening of the first day their home was on the market, he got an urgent call. It seems they got 27 showings that day, and a full price offer was on the table.

"Our home was under priced," they said. "It should have been priced higher!" So, Ken carefully reviewed the information they had at hand, including the comparable sales on which the listing price was based.

"Look," he said, "you can either be greedy and risk losing a good sale, or you can simply try to understand the dynamics of a well-listed property. You are actually priced slightly higher than the comps show. And, you need to move quickly, since you already have your replacement property under contract. These people were all waiting for another property in your neighborhood and in your price range. If you reject this offer, you could risk waiting weeks or months for another offer, and in the process lose your new home. Or, you could take this offer, recognize that you made a healthy profit, and facilitate a smooth and easy move for you and your family." They took the offer, and in less than a month, they were ensconced in their current home. Looking back, they actually laugh at their hope to have made another few thousand dollars.

Many sellers know of a home that sold for a high price in their neighborhood, and want to know why their home should not be similarly priced. But they may be unfamiliar with the particular differences between that house and their own that would justify the difference in value.

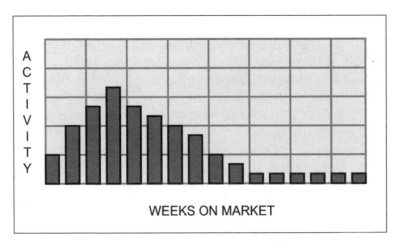

The bottom line is, don't overprice your home. Professionals know that the longer a house stays on the market, the lower the selling price will be in comparison to its original asking price. More often than not, your first offer will be your best. So if you overprice your home by 5 percent, you could end up losing 10 percent or more, and wait months to sell your home.

This leaves us with the question of how to modify the price of your home in either an up or down market to avoid overpricing. This is where a Realtor®'s advice can be invaluable. Unlike a typical seller who is only familiar with the markets that effect either the sale or purchase of their own homes, an experienced Realtor® will have the knowledge of many years of market changes and fluctuations. They will also have a database of important sales statistics which they can use to expand their knowledge base. This can turn a guessing game into an educated pricing strategy.

You may also want to consider—strategically pricing—your home. To price your home strategically, it is best to do so at the low end of the range of market values. This option can be appealing when you need to sell fast, possibly because you are moving out of the area for work, or to close on a replacement property. It is a particularly good strategy in a market where prices are falling. An underpriced property today can create an immediate reaction as opposed to becoming an overpriced property tomorrow or 30 days out when prices are lower and the home hasn't sold. In the recent past, we sold four properties where the buyer was the first and only party to see the property. These were cases where the buyers had difficulty finding the right property, the new listings were underpriced and they fit the buyer's needs perfectly. Even with full-priced offers, they got bargains. Good Realtors® check for new listings every day, and when a good one comes up, they call the buyer immediately to see the property. Underpricing can sell homes *quickly*—partly through diligent work and attention, but also as a result of a market reaction to the underpricing. This frequently results in multiple offers from competing buyers who end up paying over the asking price in order to *win* the house.

It is also important to know that there are buyers in every price range in your market just waiting for the next property listing. They've already seen everything that fits their criteria without finding the "right" home. If yours is priced right, and it fits, you could have a quick sale. However, if it is overpriced, the buyer may not see your home at all, or won't make an offer. Overpricing can cause you to lose that buyer forever.

If for some reason your house has been on the market for longer than the normal range in your market, action besides just lowering the price can and should be taken. If no one has even looked at your home, and it is in the MLS, has a lockbox, and is easy to show, you can be absolutely sure that price is the issue. Somehow, despite you and your Realtor®'s best efforts, your home is not adequately priced for your area. It may be because of a severe "buyer's market," or it may be because others in your area have taken less than full value for their homes for one reason or another. If you are unwilling to wait in order to sell your home, making adjustments to your asking price will be necessary.

If you have had people looking at your home but you still have not had any reasonable offers, you should find out what specifically is discouraging buyers. There are several ways to do so. First, your Realtor® should be getting feedback from both the buyers who saw your home, and from the Realtors® who showed it. Not all Realtors® will respond, but the feedback can be invaluable.

A word of caution—it is easy to get defensive when buyer feedback indicates "the home is overpriced" or "the floor plan doesn't work." We have had sellers say, "Well, if they don't like the price, tell them to make an offer and we'll see what we can do." The fact is that most buyers, while willing to make an offer under the asking price, do not feel comfortable "lowballing" an offer. They simply feel that negotiation would be futile.

If your home has languished on the market for several months, it may be a good time to take another look at your competition. Your Realtor® can set showings for you on competing properties, and this could serve as a reliable reality check.

Negotiating Tools

In general terms, there are two primary approaches to negotiating a sale when price alone is the major consideration. One method buyers try is to start low, with an expectation of reaching an agreed-upon price somewhat closer to the asking price. In fact, one of the jobs of the Realtor® is to try to determine your bottom line. A second approach is to make a "take it or leave it" offer. If you only want to sell at the price that you and your Realtor® have determined is fair, responding in this way is a realistic approach. Then buyers will only be able to negotiate on "cosmetic" items like the closing date or what is included in the sale. Believe it or not, we have had a number of offers accepted on that basis, but usually when the house was listed for slightly under the market value.

The vast majority of real estate transactions, when both sides are represented, should come down to what is a win/win situation where everyone feels satisfied with the conclusion. We have all dealt with buyers who "want a deal" and are unwilling to pay fair market value for any property. They are only looking for someone who is vulnerable and has to sell at any price. We usually decline to work with this type of buyer.

So, if you haven't already, you and your Realtor® should now prepare for negotiation by formulating a game plan. You should both be clear about what is vital to the sale and what you can give up. Most bottom lines should include some unnecessary items you can give up without feeling deprived, while giving the buyers the sense they won some concessions. It is also important to understand that there are many more things to negotiate besides price. In fact, there are occasions when price, although important in reeling a buyer in, is the *least* important negotiating objective.

For example, you may need a really quick close—you will lose a home you are trying to purchase and you need the sale proceeds immediately. If the buyers are renters, you may not have a problem; but if they also have a house they need to sell, it may mean convincing them to own two homes for a period of time, and you may have to concede to the offering price in order to get what you need. On the other hand, you may have just installed a brand-new lighting fixture that you would love to keep, but if it means getting your asking price, it may be worth parting with. In fact, we always recommend that you remove any items that you definitely want to keep before putting your house on the market so that you don't have to say "no" and potentially waste negotiating power on trivial items. Buyers tend to fall in love with what they can't have. Thus, it is important to know and to clearly communicate to your agent, those things that are significant.

Always try to negotiate from a position of strength. You can contribute to a stronger negotiating position by not overpricing your home. It will also help if you have taken the steps described in the next chapter to make your home as attractive as possible. And, if you are looking to buy another home, it will be to your advantage to wait until you are under contract with a buyer before you make an offer of your own unless you are in a position to own more than one home simultaneously.

Your Realtor® will also try to find out what might motivate the buyers. While it is not always possible to determine their motivations up front, it is usually worth trying. For example, if you find out that the buyers are moving from out of state and need extra moving time, you can give them the time they need in exchange for taking the appliances. If you are not in a hurry to move, and you can make a closing date or possession date concession to the buyers, don't you think they might be willing to negotiate on the price?

If you find out that the buyers are being transferred and need to move quickly, or are getting divorced, or are facing a termination of their rental lease, you will have accumulated information that is important to your negotiating position. Once you know as much as you can about the buyers' position and you and your Realtor® have a clear picture of your negotiating position, you are one step closer to selling your home with the best price and terms combination.

Another useful strategy in selling your home is to give the buyer a break. If negotiations are stalled, you might offer to throw in the the patio furniture or offer to clean the carpets after you have vacated. Small gestures can be very valuable. If a buyer is on the fence, a seller who appears willing to do something extra may have the right stuff to seal a transaction. And at the end of the day, that $500 investment on patio furniture may have saved you an extra month's delay in selling your home. Occasionally, even offering a one-year home warranty (usually around $300–$500) can do the trick.

Ira showed a Thousand Oaks home to buyers who rejected it. They viewed the home the weekend the sellers were moving out—stuff was everywhere! Several weeks later they came across the website Ira created for the sellers, and it caught their interest. One of the buyers said, "we already saw that one," but since the photos showed the home in pristine condition, they decided to see it again. They bought it and have lived there ever since.

"Staging" a Home

Ken knows a Realtor® known in the real estate industry as "Lox and Bagel." The nickname comes from the fact that he often "dresses" his listings for show, including setting the kitchen table with a lovely brunch of *synthetic* bagels topped with lox! This is called "staging" a home, a concept first developed by Barb Schwarz at www.stagedhomes.com. On Sunday mornings, when most of his open houses are held, he provides his guests with an idea of what it would be like to wake up to a beautiful brunch in that very home, which he hopes will soon be theirs. He even draws baths, complete with candles, champagne and strawberries. The bottom line is that when you view his homes, you know exactly how wonderful it could be to live there. Just as in magazine or television advertising, subtleties can make a huge difference. Your Realtor® may even get a local furniture company to display its furniture in a new home where construction is just complete.

We compare this to a department store window where professional designers or decorators have "set" the stage for creating the highest level of customer appeal and interest. Imagine the reaction if the designer or decorator hung an Armani suit or Vera Wang dress in the window on a wire hanger with a bare light bulb above compared to creating a positive image for the buyers to observe! Ira was skeptical at first of the usefulness of staging a home. Then he saw a home before, and after, staging. He's sure the seller's $3,000–5,000 investment paid off multifold.

You may not be able to do all of the things recommended above, for financial reasons or otherwise, but any of the steps you can take will put your home in a better selling position.

It is important to realize that when a potential buyer views your home, you have your one and only chance to make the right impression. Indeed, the first impression may also be the last. You may know that the dishes are usually washed and the lawn raked, but a potential homeowner only knows what they see on that first viewing. So before you cost yourself time and money, make sure your house is "dressed and ready" for sale!

6. Pre-Sale Preparation

Thanks for the excellent service you gave us in selling our home. It was truly amazing experience! First off, you were right in suggesting that we get a termite report before the property went on the market so that we could see exactly what we were potentially working against from the buyers' perspective. Samia, it was truly a pleasure having you represent us. You gave us first class treatment from day one beginning with your presentation of your services. We felt that you had gone all out even though we have been neighbors. You were there for us the whole way through, called with updates, and handled more than I think another agent would have.

—Hilda and Kirk Hasserjian, Intel

Your pre-sale preparation is key to your success not just in selling your home, but in getting the best price with the least inconvenience. Most sellers will enlist the help of a real estate sales professional, and that is the best place to start. Find a good Realtor® early in the process and they will help you months in advance with decisions about inspections, repairs, staging, and so on. Take your time with this important task. Interview, check references, do your homework, and then enlist their help in the preparation stage of selling your home.

Your Realtor® can help you make a list of needed improvements and repairs. Take care of the obvious things. Most buyers will want a pest report (termites, dry rot, and beetles) and a list of other basic repairs made (leak free roof, no plumbing leaks, and safe electrical conditions, for instance) and one of our local contracts demands it. There are many good reasons for a seller to do pre-sale inspections. One is that if the buyer goes into contract on a home knowing its condition, that buyer is far less likely to back out later. When buyers do back out and a home sells again, it often sells for less than the amount it sold for the first time.

Another reason for pre-sale inspections is to avoid the experience of "writing a blank check" for repairs. One of our contracts requires that there are no leaks, that every system in the home is operational, that there are no wood destroying pests, and so on. If you sell and do not know the exact condition of your home, you may be promising repairs for which you don't even know the cost! Do your inspections before accepting a contract. Find out the costs of repairs. Not only will it keep you from "writing a blank check" later, it will improve your bottom line most of the time. For instance, if your bathroom floor has dry rot from water splashing out of the tub or shower area, you can do the repair and then sell a more attractive home that boasts a new floor. If you waited until a buyer was in contract to learn that the repair was needed, you would have sold at a lower price and then had the unpleasant surprise of seeing your bottom line shrink while the buyer enjoyed a new floor at your expense.

So hire qualified inspectors to do whatever inspections are needed to know what the basic condition of your home is. For single-family homes, this usually includes a pest, roof, and property inspection at a minimum. If you're in a condo, it might simply be a pest and property inspection (sometimes homeowners associations (HOA) do not cover decks). And if there are issues with various components of your property, you may need those inspected too: foundations, pools, and chimneys for instance. We always recommend a chimney cleaning and inspection—we are in earthquake country and find a lot of broken chimneys upon inspection.

After selecting an agent and determining the condition of your property (fixing what you want and deciding to exclude other repairs or improvements once you do get an offer), you should be able to work with your agent to decide on a pricing strategy. Pricing mistakes can be serious, but are correctable. Know that you may have to revisit and refine the pricing strategy as you get close to going on the market. Remember that conditions such as the economy, competition or lack thereof, interest rates, and so on can change.

Next you'll want to completely fill out all required disclosure forms. California is a disclosure–heavy state due to a lot of litigation. Your best strategy is to disclose, disclose, disclose. And to make sure you do a thorough job, do it before a buyer is waiting and you're under a time crunch. Take your time and be thorough. Review it with your agent to make sure you are clear and have covered everything. Again, if a buyer can learn about the condition of the property before writing an offer, that buyer is far less likely to back out of the sale later. So make the condition of your property known upfront!

Lastly, work with your agent on staging. We provide a lot of information on that later in the chapter because it is so important. Once your home is "dressed and ready for sale," your Realtor® can arrange the photography and videography of the house so that when it goes on the market you can launch an impressive marketing campaign.

Dressed and Ready for Sale

Buying a home can be one of the most emotional purchases a person or family makes. A buyer may see that perfect bay window with the window seat they've always dreamed of and know that your home has to be theirs. So, in order to have the most successful experience selling your home, you must appeal to the *emotions* of potential buyers.

The reality is that what your home looks like matters—a lot! Deep down, most buyers want a home that they can move into without any work to be done, regardless of what they can really afford. No matter the age of your house, your job is to make it appear as good as possible without wasting money. Obviously, if your house was perfect you probably wouldn't want to move, but the point is to make it as appealing as possible.

Dos and Don'ts

When you are selling your home, there are some very simple and inexpensive things that you can do, or that you should avoid. Remember, you have a very valuable item to sell. So like a sophisticated salesperson, you should make sure that the product you are offering is useful and appealing. By following these 10 simple tips, you can not only increase the sale price of your home, but hopefully ensure a quick sale as well. To illustrate, consider the following points:

Tip 1: Get rid of any and all clutter. Piles of books and magazines, snow-globe collections and bags of recycling can be such a negative distraction that potential buyers might walk right out before passing the entry hall. The goal is to make your house spotless. The less clutter there is, the more open and spacious your home will appear and the more likely it is that the buyer will also be able to imagine themselves and their things in your home. Too much furniture and too many knick-knacks always make a room look smaller than it is. Don't forget the closets and the garage! Storage space is an important concern of many buyers, so the less cluttered these spaces are, the more space buyers think they are getting. Don't wait until you start packing to donate those unneeded items—just do it now! It gives you one less thing to worry about later and at the same time, adds value to your home. There's no need to make major changes because most homeowners want to decorate themselves. You want to give buyers a spacious and clean blank canvas so they can imagine their own painting!

Sometimes, nothing can be more detrimental to selling a home than the aforementioned clutter and mess. A friend of ours, Allyson, once listed a property that had been sitting on the market for five months for just this reason. The sellers were a young couple with two small children. As a result, the house was filled with excess furniture and toys. Our colleague suggested that they rent a storage locker for the over-abundant furnishings in an effort to create a greater sense of space. Thankfully they took the advice. They ended up selling the house at full price the very first day it was listed! The most amazing part of this success was that our colleague did *not* reduce the price upon relisting the home. The only investment on the seller's part was their time and the minimal cost of a storage facility.

Tip 2: Avoid air fresheners. To prospective buyers, air fresheners seem like cover ups. You are better off making sure that your home has been well aired out, particularly if you are a smoker. Try using strategically placed fresh flowers to add a touch of ambience as well as a fresh scent, or bake fresh cookies or bread.

Tip 3: Make sure that your home is as inviting as possible. This means turning off the television and any other distracting electronic device. Instead, try using soft music to set the tone. You might also want inviting lighting. Make sure you have high-watt bulbs in dark rooms and soft lighting in areas where you want to detract attention.

Tip 4: Make sure pets and children are not around or are unobtrusive when your house is being shown to prospective buyers. It is best to assume that buyers don't have pets or children and let them ask questions about how a home can accommodate their needs if necessary. The bottom line is that if a buyer is allergic to cats or dogs, your beloved pet may drive them out before giving your home a chance.

Tip 5: You should avoid potentially offensive items. Samia recently showed a home to a prospective buyer, Mary, a lovely lady with a quiet personality who was not only vegetarian, but vegan. She not only wouldn't eat meat, she wouldn't eat anything that came from an animal, like milk or cheese, and she would not wear leather or fur.

You can imagine her dismay when she walked into the bedroom of a nice three-bedroom, two-bathroom, split-level home and was confronted with a picture of Ozzy Osbourne biting off a bat's head. There was no sale that day. We always check our listings for offensive items to make sure it will appeal to the majority of perspective buyers. First impressions count!

Ken recalls a townhome he once marketed that was dreary, dark and depressing. It had languished on the market for months with another agent. He suggested that the seller replace the worn gold carpets with new, moderately priced neutral carpets and paint the gold walls white. The seller reluctantly invested about $2,000 in the process but was thrilled when she ended up netting $12,000 more than any previous offer they had entertained—and the whole process was accomplished within weeks!

Tip 8: Make sure that you don't leave your car in the driveway. This is a little-known secret of the trade. When a buyer pulls up they should see the home, not your cars. Let them feel like the driveway is theirs, and maybe even visualize themselves coming home. If you can't park your car in the garage because of clutter, reread Tip 1.

Tip 9: You should also make sure that any important papers, prescription drugs, and valuables are put away in a safe place. The reality is that buyers are strangers that you are letting into your home. Although a Realtor® will always be there to show them around, it is best not to take chances with your private and valuable items. Besides, some buyers, such as families, wander in different directions, and it is impossible for a Realtor® to monitor all individuals all the time. It is not unheard of for drug addicts to occasionally visit houses with the intent of stealing prescription drugs for resale or personal use. Having an agent present when you are showing your home adds safety and can ensure that prospective buyers have all the information they need to make an offer on your home. Add to that your knowledgeable Realtor®, readily available to share information through good marketing, and savvy buyers will have the most likely combination of influences designed to produce the results you want.

Tip 10: Be sure to follow the **Rule of Three "Cs"**. Keep your home as **C**lean as possible, as **C**lutterfree as possible and as **C**olorless as possible. This simple rule, if followed, will ensure that your home appeals to the greatest number of prospective buyers.

Making the Buyer Comfortable

Potential buyers may be entering their future home and can't help but emotionally connect with the surroundings. You can take advantage of this. Samia suggests making an invitation. Take a card and place it on the coffee table. Say something like, "Please sit and make yourself comfortable for a bit, as this just might be your new home. We've enjoyed living here, and I think you will too."

You can also make coffee or bake cookies. This is not only a kind gesture, but adds pleasing, comfortable aromas.

Another useful tool is to give a list of your favorite features to your agent. This way your Realtor® can draw buyers to the best parts of your home. What made you want to buy your home is likely a selling point for prospective buyers. The more your Realtor® points out to potential buyers, the more comfortable they will feel, and the less time they will need to spend learning about the home for themselves. It helps them sell the sizzle, not just the steak!

One area over which you may have little control is your neighborhood. Regardless, we all know how important a factor this is in buying a home. You can team up with neighbors to form a neighborhood organization or Neighborhood Watch program. Prospective buyers may be delighted to know that even though you are leaving, they are moving into a neighborhood that cares.

It is also important to realize that in order to get the best price for your home, it should appeal to as many people as possible. This usually means keeping the decorating, interior and exterior, as minimal and neutral as possible. Remember that what suited you in your home will not necessarily suit the majority of potential buyers. The following story illustrates this point.

A couple, both artists, had decorated their home with amazing artwork painted directly onto the walls throughout the house—lovely work, but definitely *not* something that would have vast market appeal. After much discussion they finally agreed to repaint some of the most "impressive" walls white. However, they still insisted on keeping the turquoise trim surrounding the exterior of their windows. When the house didn't sell, their Realtor's® feedback indicated that there were still issues with the decorating and color. In response, the sellers decided to lower their price by $10,000, hoping to produce an offer. At their Realtor's® suggestion, "humor me," he said, they finally agreed to first repaint the turquoise trim on the outside white, a minimal expense as compared to a radical price reduction. The house sold within a week and the sellers never had to reduce their price, which ultimately netted thousands of dollars more than they were prepared to accept.

Today's homebuyer is looking for "character." Just as popcorn ceilings are out, natural wood floors are in. If you are going to spend money on renovating parts of your home, there are two places where your investment will have the greatest payback: the kitchen and the bathroom. Replacing kitchen counters and floors alone can brighten up a dated kitchen. A simple counter replacement from formica to a granite slab can be a huge plus. Even granite tile will make a more pleasing look than regular tile. In fact, granite looks so good, that Ira & Carol have installed granite countertops in Casita Adela (named after Ira's mother), their new family room. There are multiple resources at large home improvement stores that offer very price competitive solutions. Likewise, bathroom remodels can be moderately priced and can substantially update your home. You don't need to take any of these steps to sell your home, but be aware of what buyers will be looking for and how you can best meet their needs. Just making your home sparkling clean can make that huge difference. Sellers must consider these factors and decide for themselves how much time and money they can invest in the final sale price of their home.

Exterior

As previously mentioned, first impressions are important, and the first thing that prospective buyers will see is the outside of your home. The exterior not only speaks for itself, but it tells potential buyers what they can expect to find inside. The reality is that if the exterior of your home is in a bad state, many buyers will just keep on driving. If you drove up to a house with peeling paint, dead plants and falling rain gutters, you wouldn't expect the inside to be taken care of, would you? See our checklist at the end of the chapter for ideas that will assure the outside of your home is as well dressed as the inside—dressed for success!

Remember, you only get one chance to make a first impression and that begins with the outside of your home, so landscaping should be groomed, walks and driveways should be free of weeds and chipping paint, toys should not adorn the front yard and your front door should look great. Your potential buyer will have a significant amount of time to observe these things while their agent gains access to your home.

Amenities

The most common problem we see after a closing is that the seller takes an item from the property that the buyer assumed was part of the sale. This goes back to an important point that we discussed earlier: Make sure that items you want to keep are either removed from the house before you show it to prospective buyers, or stipulate in the listing sheet what stays and what goes. Ultimately, there are some items that will automatically become part of the property once title is passed to the buyer, regardless of whether you assumed they were yours to keep. This is referred to as the *law of fixtures.*

The law of fixtures basically says that fixtures are part of the property and cannot be removed. Fixtures include anything that is permanently attached to the property by attachments such as bolts, screws, nails, plumbing or alarm wiring. Some items are easy to understand as fixtures, such as counters, sinks, or flooring. But some areas are more complicated. For example, a built-in dishwasher is a fixture since it can't just be unplugged and removed, while a refrigerator or clothes washer is not if you can simply unplug and remove it. Other appliances can be considered both, so they must be laid out in contract. Similarly, window treatments, or book shelves or mirrors bolted to the wall for earthquake safety are considered fixtures if they are screwed or bolted in. So you can take curtains, but not the rod if it is bolted to the wall. Other appliances may be considered both, so they must be laid out in the contract.

Another common area of confusion is lighting. If light fixtures are bolted to the wall or ceiling they are part of the sale, even including expensive chandeliers and antiques. The only way to avoid a potential problem is to remove these items and replace them with inexpensive fixtures before showing your home. Unlike nonfixtures, otherwise known as personal property (refrigerators, washers and dryers), a buyer does not even have to request these items in the contract, as fixtures are included in the contract as part of the sale.

If your home has a dated stove or refrigerator, it may be worthwhile to buy a new one before you show your home. This runs slightly counter to the rule that you shouldn't show items that you intend to keep, but here there is a good reason. Think of your kitchen as a showroom. Unlike lighting fixtures, buyers generally know that these appliances are not necessarily included in the sale. The cost of these appliances is typically around $1,500 or so for a stove or refrigerator, and it will make a significant difference. Nice appliances can show prospective buyers how contemporary and updated your kitchen can look. Dated appliances really make a kitchen look old. Even if your buyers insist on keeping the appliances (make sure you are adequately compensated. Remember, the seller should always stipulate what stays and what goes), the overall look may still ensure a quicker sale at a better price.

Real Problems

There may be some real problems with your house that need to be repaired before you sell it. Major "as-is" fixer-uppers can be hard to sell. In fact, you should never spend money on cosmetic repairs unless you know that your home is structurally sound. If there are genuine problems with your home, you should either spend the money to address them, or understand that you will have to sell it as a fixer-upper for a reduced price.

Leaks Don't Lie

Ken's Story:

Some years ago, before I was a Realtor®, I was a private investigator. I received a call from an attorney who represented the Gordons, a couple who had recently bought a great old home.

It seems the Gordons, during the moving-in process, filled the garage with dozens of boxes that contained an old and rare book collection they had been adding to for years. The first weekend after they had moved in, before they finished unpacking, there was a huge rainstorm.

The Gordons never anticipated what would happen during that storm. It rained inside the garage, destroying a significant amount of their rare book collection along with lots of other household items. The Gordons were away at the time, so the situation progressed unimpeded. They were devastated when they returned home. Of course, they had had a professional home inspection when they were under contract to purchase the home, and the inspector did not indicate the presence of any roof leaks. They contacted their agent, who had recommended the inspector, and asked for assistance. She contacted the sellers' agent, who professed no knowledge, then purportedly contacted the seller, who also claimed innocence. The Gordons, in their extreme frustration, hired an attorney, who contacted me to conduct a thorough investigation.

The resulting lawsuit named several people: the sellers, the sellers' agent, the home inspector, the buyers' agent, and the two brokers, and here is why each was culpable.

The Sellers

My investigation revealed that the sellers had experienced roof leaks as a matter of course for several years. It was a Spanish-style tile roof and very expensive to repair or replace. I had located the roofing company that had performed repairs to the roof through the years. I obtained a statement from the owner of the company that, two years prior to the sale, he had told the sellers that he refused to do any more repairs to the roof because the patchwork was not working. The roof needed to be replaced. That disclosure to the sellers was also in writing from the roofing company. The Sellers Property Disclosure, given to the buyers during the contract period, indicated that the roof was sound and had no leaks.

The Sellers' Agent

The sellers' agent was well known. She'd been in business for many years and had a reputation for specializing in high-end listings in this neighborhood. She was known for staging her homes so that they would sell quicker. That is, she would instruct her sellers to paint and do other cosmetic work to make the house look its best, and she would even lend expensive furniture when it would help make the home look luxurious. When I met with her and her broker, she denied any knowledge of roof leaks or other problems pertaining to the house. I was able to determine, however, that she had instructed the sellers to paint parts of the interior of the home. I later learned from other sources that she had specifically noted water stains on the living room, dining room and other walls, and ordered those painted so the water stains would not be noticed by visiting prospective buyers.

The Home Inspector

Before meeting with the original home inspector, I hired another, and we went through the home in some detail. Among other things, we noted that in the attic, the sellers had placed sheets of plastic, each of which showed dried watermarks. It was clear that the sheets of plastic were meant to capture water leaking from the roof. When I interviewed the home inspector, he admitted that he had never gone into the attic (even to inspect the insulation). He also admitted he had no money and no insurance and didn't even own a home. He said, "So sue me. I'll just go out of business." In fact, he was not bonded or insured and didn't even have any formal training.

The Buyers' Agent

Of all the parties, this woman was the most innocent. She truly felt she had done her job and was straightforward in her interview with me. She was also fairly new in the business, with little more than a year of experience at the time she worked with the Gordons. However, she had made a serious mistake. She had recommended a home inspector without having checked out his credentials or reputation. The simple action of checking with her broker or other agents in her office to make sure her buyers had a truly professional inspector could have prevented this entire incident despite the efforts on the parts of the sellers and their agent to hide the evidence.

The Brokers

Regardless of the direct liability and culpability of the agents involved, they work for, and are under the supervision of, their brokers. In both cases, the brokers either failed to train their agents properly or failed to supervise their actions effectively. Hence, they were named in the lawsuit as well. In fact, this is another good reason to work with a Realtor®.

The Result

The Gordons won their lawsuit. However, it took more than a year, and in the meantime, they had to finance a complete roof replacement on their own. It was difficult to accurately ascertain the value of the rare books they lost, so the amount they collected for lost goods was far less than what they felt they should have gotten. Of course, they received no compensation for the psychological pain and suffering they endured, nor for the time lost from work pursuing the lawsuit. So, in spite of the fact that some justice was eventually served, no one came out a true winner, and the entire mess could have been avoided with good representation and a little honesty.

Samia's Story

A few years ago, one of Samia's's clients, Tim, listed a rather old Queen Anne–style home that had been in his family for generations. He had recently inherited the home and wasn't particularly interested in fixing it up or living in it, so he decided to put it on the market. He informed his original Realtor®, whom we'll call Joe, that he didn't know much about the condition of the house, but that he did remember that the bathroom on the second floor had flooded a few years before, leaking through the ceiling and eventually damaging two of the downstairs bedrooms. Because the carpet had been replaced and the walls repainted, there was no visible sign of the incident.

Joe advised Tim not to say anything to avoid scaring away potential buyers. Taking Joe's advice, he accepted a full-price offer and never made any mention of the water damage.

During the inspection, the water damage was discovered and the buyers not only backed out, but they threatened both Tim and Joe with lawsuits for failing to disclose known damage to the property.

As it turned out, Tim came to Samia's office. She not only helped Tim with the mess that Joe had created, but put Tim's family home back on the market with full disclosure of the water damage, and listed it for only $10,000 less than the original asking price. Although it took a few months to sell, Samia finally sold the home to a handyman and his wife because they knew that they could make the necessary repairs for under $3,000 and were happy to have saved some money! There is always a buyer for every home; the important thing is finding the *right* buyer.

It's always a great idea to pay for a home inspection and pest control report before putting your home on the market.

Start with your own home inspection. A visual inspection will help you pinpoint potentially serious issues so that you can have them assessed by a specialist.

You should also be aware that once you know about defects, you are legally obligated to disclose them to potential buyers. You and your agent must disclose any *known* material defects in your property. Even if you are selling your house "as is" and the buyer must accept any conditions as part of the sale, they still must be fully disclosed!

Insurance

As long as you plan to sell your home, you need to make sure the home is insurable.

Recently, a Realtor® friend reported receiving a termination notice from her insurance company. She had been insured with the same company for more than 25 years and had never filed a claim. However, the insurance company just found out that she lived more than ten miles from a fire station.

Another Realtor® friend received a notice from one of his sellers who had recently listed a home for sale. The notice included a copy of a letter received from his insurance company. His insurance was being cancelled because his home was on the market for sale; the insurance company stated that having one's home for sale presented greater risk due to the fact that strangers would be going through it.

It should be noted that the National Association of Realtors® (NAR) and its state associations are fighting for legislation that would prevent such arbitrary rules by insurance companies.

Any buyer who will require financing will also require hazard insurance, otherwise known as homeowner's insurance. Their lender will not provide financing without it. If you are selling a condominium, townhouse or other property that is considered a *common interest community*, this section may not apply. If the property has a homeowners' association that provides insurance on all the units, a buyer will not have to purchase their own.

Insurance covers a number of things, the most disastrous of which being total loss of the home by fire or other calamity. Homeowner's insurance also provides liability coverage in the event that someone is injured on the property, and it covers in the event of loss from theft or other smaller mishaps. Interestingly, however, some of the things that most dramatically affect homeowners are being decreased or eliminated from insurance coverage, such as coverage for mold and water leaks. There are two primary reasons that insurance companies are refusing to underwrite insurance on new purchases:

1. You, the seller has either filed a claim, or simply called about a problem, and the insurance company no longer wishes to insure or reinsure the home. Your insurance company could refuse to renew, or the refusal could come from a different company that has been contacted by you or the buyer. The property may have had water problems, whether from leaky roofs, broken pipes or runoff, and the insurance company feels it may happen again or the property may have mold. The interesting thing is that you may not have even filed a claim. You may simply have called to see if a situation would be covered and if you *should* file a claim. But overall, companies feel that properties that have experienced past claims are more likely to experience future claims. The property now becomes, for all practical purposes, uninsurable.

2. The buyer may have had claims on a prior residence that makes the buyer, in the eyes of insurance underwriters, uninsurable. It could be because of similar problems noted above. It could be because a company had to pay a claim since the buyer's previous home was poorly maintained. Overall, companies state that buyers who have filed past claims are more likely to file future claims. Whatever the reason, the buyer becomes uninsurable.

Insurance companies claim a number of reasons for the current crisis. They point to the $40+ billion in losses in the World Trade Center terrorist attack and to major losses from natural disasters such as Hurricane Katrina. They point to the surge of mold-related claims and call attention to aggressive low pricing in the past that resulted in major losses. What they do not point to, but studies have shown may be the actual reason for their loss of profits, are the losses they have suffered on their stock market investments.

The warning is clear: You can no longer take property insurance for granted. The buyer must apply for and obtain homeowner's insurance at the earliest possible date in a transaction. Then, if denied by one company, there is at least time for them to shop for other coverage. You might also seek out an insurance broker who works with multiple lines. A broker would have a better idea of where to place an application based on either credit scores or claims history.

Ira and Carol had a client who bought a beautiful home in the Berkeley Hills. Ira referred his buyer to a superb insurance agent. The buyer had a good working relationship with his Southern California agent, so they decided to continue using him. When Ira received an email from the insurance agent asking strange questions (Are there any chandeliers in the home? Are there any built-in bookshelves? What kind of floors are in the kitchen?), he told the buyer that the agent was looking for ways to *not* issue an insurance policy. Once the insurance agent got the answers to the questions, however, he told the buyers that they would insure the home.

About a week later, after the buyers had removed their insurance contingency, the insurance agent called to tell them that they had been turned down. Fortunately, Ira had such a great working relationship with his insurance agent, the buyers were issued a policy within a few hours!

What Is a C.L.U.E. Report?

A claims history report on a seller's residence (called C.L.U.E. for Comprehensive Loss Underwriting Exchange) can be obtained from ChoicePoint, an online identification and credential verification service. Through their ChoiceTrust program, they manage and maintain information about claims filed on properties in the United States (www.choicetrust.com). The report will show all claims filed in the past five years, including the nature and amount of each settlement. Examples could range from water or fire damage to dog bites. About 90 percent of all insurers nationally participate in C.L.U.E. and a good insurance broker will most likely know those that don't.

C.L.U.E. reports are available on properties, not individuals, so when a buyer makes an offer on a property, they will have a clause requiring you to obtain a C.L.U.E. report. It will cost you approximately $20, and you can pay and download the report online or request it by mail. If you find your home is determined to be uninsurable, it's much better to know in advance so you have time to check insurability with other companies. Mortgage lenders require insurance, so if you are stuck with a property that is uninsurable, you would most likely have to attract a cash buyer to purchase the home.

Insist as a counter to any offer, that the buyer immediately contact a lender and have them check the buyer's insurance scores to make sure they are not at risk of being unable to obtain insurance. And once an offer becomes a contract, make sure the buyer applies for and obtains insurance immediately. If they have been denied coverage and received a letter from an insurance company, they can obtain a free copy of their scores for review from ChoicePoint (www.ConsumerDisclosure.com). The point to emphasize is that you should obtain a C.L.U.E. report immediately upon listing your property for sale. Then, you will either have time to address any problems that come up, or relax with the knowledge that there will be no concerns that could prevent a sale.

This issue of insurance has become so important that the National Association of REALTORS® has appointed an Insurance Task Force to address the growing problem. The task force has already put forth recommendations for state associations to begin working on legislation, to educate their members and to discover other ways of handling the problem.

Checklist for Home Preparation

Begin with the Exterior

1. Keep the lawn mowed. A well-manicured lawn, neatly trimmed shrubs, and cleanly swept sidewalks create a good first impression.

2. Be sure to fertilize your grass to make it look lush and green.

3. Trim or cut back overgrown shrubs.

4. Paint the house if necessary. (If you do decide to paint your house, drive through new neighborhoods and choose a contemporary, neutral color. Don't paint your house the same old color it was in 1970.)

5. Clean stains and oil from walkways, sidewalks, and driveways. A badly stained driveway suggests that the house may not have been well maintained. If it's painted and it's chipped or peeling, repaint. Pressure wash patios, walkways, and driveways.

6. Replace cracked or broken windows and torn screens.

7. Hose down the exterior of your house to get rid of annoying cobwebs and dead bugs.

8. Make sure the entry light and doorbell are in good working order.

9. Inspect the roof, chimney, and gutters. Make repairs and paint as necessary.

10. Repaint the front door. A new coat of paint suggests a well-cared-for home. Remove the screen door to show off the newly-painted door.

11. Put a fresh coat of paint on your mailbox.

12. Place a pot of fresh flowers by the front door or along the walk in the spring or summer.

Now Let's Look at the Interior

1. Begin with a full housecleaning from top to bottom. Clean out closets and throw away unused items. Make sure that clothes are hung neatly and shoes are tidily arranged. Eliminating clutter makes your home look more spacious.

2. Make sure the walls are clean and free of smudges and fingerprints. Give them a fresh coat of paint if washing doesn't do the trick.

3. Arrange furniture to make your rooms appear more spacious. Get rid of badly worn furniture or place it in storage.

4. Wash the windows, inside and out!

5. Wash or replace the curtains.

6. Clean the carpets and wax the floors.

7. Repair any sticking doors.

8. Fix leaky faucets and clean the water stains from the sinks, toilets and shower doors.

9. Make sure all light fixtures are in good working order, and replace burned-out light bulbs with the highest wattage allowable for the fixture.

10. The kitchen is the most important room in your house. Make it bright and inviting. Wash the walls and cabinets or give them a new coat of paint if necessary. Clean the vent hood. If the floor is badly worn, consider replacing it.

11. Make the bathrooms sparkle! Repair old caulk in showers and tubs. Place fresh towels in the bathrooms.

12. Clean the bedrooms and replace faded curtains and bedspreads.

13. Clean the basement and the garage. Get rid of items you no longer use or put them in storage. Make sure there is plenty of light in the basement.

14. If you have a basement that is dark and gloomy, consider giving the walls and floor a coat of white paint.

15. Make sure your house smells fresh and clean. Nothing is a bigger turnoff to a buyer than a smelly dog bed, dirty litter box, or nicotine.

16. If there is a wood-burning fireplace, have the chimney cleaned. This is not only a safety measure—soot has an odor!

7. Screening Prospective Buyers

We'd like to express to Carol and Ira how pleasant it was to work with you both. From the first time we met, you were completely reliable, intensely involved, and exceedingly competent in each step involved in the sale of our Berkeley home! Your creativity helped us to understand and take advantage of the prevailing market situation, and guided us ably into a contract that completely blew our socks off! We appreciated your dealings with our relocation agency, which helped to eliminate the stress involved with a big move. And most of all, we appreciated your sense of humor and your sound advice throughout the sales process. We will highly recommend you to our friends and family.

—Andrea and Michael Scharff

Motivation

The motivation for selling your home will be a substantial factor in determining the kind of offer that you are looking for. For example, if you need to sell your home because you have been offered a job in a new state, you may be willing to list your home at a lower price with fewer conditions. This will make the terms of the offer the important selling point and most likely afford you a broader range of buyers than if you are merely selling in order to buy a bigger home. Likewise, a buyer looking for an investment property may want different things than one who is looking for a home for their family. Knowing both your motivation and the motivation of your prospective buyers can help the negotiating process. There are many types of buyers with many different financial backgrounds, and sometimes a buyer with a 10 percent down payment can be just as good as an all-cash buyer.

Conventional Financing

When selling your home, you will likely be familiar with some of the basics of financing based upon your own experiences as a buyer. However, there are some important aspects of financing about which you should be knowledgeable in order to ensure that your perfect buyer can actually afford your home. How the buyer intends to pay for your home, and whether or not they are qualified for financing, is really the most important aspect of the entire sales transaction. We all know that without the money, there is no sale.

There are four primary sources for financing the purchase of a home: banks, credit unions, mortgage bankers, and mortgage brokers. Most people are aware that banks, savings and loans, and credit unions loan money directly to the buyer from their own pool of funds, usually based on customer deposits. The individuals that work for the bank are usually called *loan officers*. Loan officers are often paid commission in addition to their salary, which provides their incentive to obtain loan applications.

Mortgage bankers are also direct lenders and use their own funds, or those of wealthy investors, but they usually do not keep the loan in their portfolio. They will often sell off the loan to a government-sanctioned major home lender like Freddie Mac or Fannie Mae. You might not even know if your loan has been sold, as mortgage bankers often continue to service a loan by mailing statements and collecting payments.

Mortgage brokers shop around for buyers of loans, searching for the lender with the program or interest rate that fits their client's situation. They take the application and can apply to dozens of lenders like banks and mortgage bankers, and they act as intermediaries between borrowers and lenders. They can't control interest rates or terms and are usually paid by both the buyer and the lender through closing fees or points. The points paid to buy the loan are often the same as going directly through the lender. One point equals 1 percent of the loan amount. Regardless of whether a buyer uses a broker or a banker, the key is making sure that your buyer has obtained adequate financing assurances prior to making an offer on your home.

Prequalification and Preapproval

The terms prequalification and preapproval are often used by buyers and their agents. It is extremely important that you know the significant difference between them. The difference is *thinking* you can afford to buy a home as opposed to having the bank say you qualify. A prequalification letter says the buyer earns enough money to buy a home in a certain price range. Unfortunately, this is based on information given to a bank or mortgage broker by the buyer over the phone. The lender has not verified the buyer's income or run a credit report. Therefore, they do not know if the buyer's credit is wonderful or terrible, or if they can secure a loan to fit the buyer's budget.

On the other hand, if a buyer has a preapproval letter, the lender has checked the buyer's credit and basic information on their income and debts, and knows approximately the size of a loan for which the buyer will qualify. Obviously, you want to make sure that the buyer is not just prequalified to buy your home, but that they are actually preapproved in writing. We highly recommend a preapproval letter as the preferred procedure.

Many lenders also perform "desktop underwriting." If the buyer's credit is good enough, and if it appears their income, debt ratios and/or FICO scores (see Chapter 11) are strong, the lender can submit a loan application immediately by computer and then receive, almost immediately, an answer from an underwriter. It will usually come in the form of full loan approval up to a certain amount, subject to an appraisal of the property value, the title report search and a ratified contract. This is, of course, the best kind of information to receive from a buyer.

When you enter into a contract with a buyer there will likely be a deadline by which they must have full loan approval. If they do not obtain full loan approval by the contract contingency deadline, the buyer or seller may terminate the contract. If the buyer does not terminate the contract, they will be obligated to purchase the home or they may lose their earnest money deposit (see Chapter 8). This helps to ensure that your interests are protected.

Prequalification Letter

The following is a prequalification clause already found in most standard contracts today.

Within 7 (or ___ Days) after acceptance, Buyer shall provide Seller a letter from lender or mortgage loan broker stating that, based on a review of Buyer's written application and credit report, Buyer is prequalified or preapproved for the new loan specified in 2C above.

Creative Financing

Buyers who have trouble getting financing through the normal programs may need to get creative. Some ideas our borrowers like are the *NIV* or *no-doc* loan. With enough money down, usually 20 percent but sometimes only 10 percent, buyers can get one of these loans. NIV stands for "no income verification" and designates a loan where the lender feels secure enough with the size of the down payment and/or the credit history of the borrower that they don't concern themselves with verifying the income stated on the loan application. The lender may simply verify that the buyer is employed and that they actually have the resources necessary to cover the down payment and closing costs. A no-doc loan is a loan where the lender does not require documentation of either income or assets (assets in this case being the money to cover down payment and closing costs). Both of these loans will have a higher interest rate, as much as 1 to 2 percent higher than conforming loans. But when buyers can't secure normal financing, these are still good loans to consider.

Many Realtors® have also identified certain people who have money to invest, and who would like to earn somewhat more than the prevailing 30-year Treasury rate. For 1 or 2 percent above the current 30-year interest rate, they are often willing to finance a smaller loan themselves. Sometimes such loans have balloon payments, meaning that after a period of time (perhaps five years), the entire amount of the principal becomes due even though the loan may be amortized over 30 years. For people who have had credit problems but can demonstrate they are making efforts to clean up their credit, a loan such as this will often get them to the point where they can get conventional refinancing long before a balloon payment becomes due. When a buyer has very little cash to put down, a private lender may take other collateral instead, such as cars or business equipment.

There are many types of creative financing. All of them carry more risk to the buyer than normal conventional financing, and most will cost more in terms of interest rates. But there is really no risk to you as long as the buyer has been preapproved. When you are looking for the right buyer, knowing that they have secured financing, even if through unconventional means, will ensure that your sale will be successful. Sometimes it's the only way to make a transaction work, and if so, you shouldn't be afraid to sell to someone who is using creative financing. Just make sure you ask a lot of questions and have your Realtor® at your side.

8. You Have Received Offers. . .Now What?

Our home was on the market one day! The most important trait is trust. Pete was great and I felt he supported and represented us well. He came up with a price and gave us a lot of imformation from history on other homes. Everything went well. We would surely use him again.

—Richard and Annette Emerson

Once a potential buyer has decided that they are interested in purchasing your home, their agent will prepare the actual offer, called a *purchase agreement.* The offer will then be submitted to you and your agent to be evaluated. This is often done in person, particularly if it is not a multiple-offer situation. A personal meeting has the advantage of allowing you to size up the other agent, to ask any questions about the offer or the buyer and to get an immediate answer. If the buyer's agent has an overwhelming demeanor (pushy) and you are timid, or if there are a lot of offers to review, this may not be the best approach. Ask your agent for guidance. Some buyer's agents will simply fax the offer over to your agent without calling first. This is not a good sign of professionalism! The way you receive the offer may tell you a lot about how the escrow period will go. In addition to a signed Agency Disclosure and the Purchase Agreement, the potential buyer will also present you with a prequalification or preapproval letter from their lender and a deposit, also called *earnest money,* to signify that they are serious about buying the home, that they intend to perform as promised under the offer and that they will come to closing with the balance of the money needed to close the purchase.

The initial deposit, or earnest money, is usually between 1 and 3 percent (though sometimes less) of the purchase price. The reason for this is the Liquidated Damages clause in the contract. If the buyer and seller agree to Liquidated Damages, and the buyer later defaults (the buyer decides not to complete the purchase after all contingencies have been removed), the maximum amount of "Liquidated Damages" the seller can hope to keep is the 3 percent deposit. In some areas, agents expect the full 3 percent deposit at the time the offer is presented. Others look for the 3 percent deposit either upfront or in two installments, with an increased deposit when contingencies are removed. Sometimes the buyer simply does not have 3 percent in liquid funds and it cannot be done, but generally, Realtors® will advise sellers to expect offers with deposits of 3 percent.

Every few years we experience a very strong "seller's market" in which there is a severe shortage of available housing to purchase compared to the number of buyers trying to get into homes. This can be a tricky time for both buyers and sellers. Offers may be written with the full 3 percent deposit upfront, "as is," or with very short contingency time frames (days for inspecting the property, getting full loan approval and so on), or with the elimination of certain contingencies altogether. (This is not an all-inclusive list of strategies that buyer's agents may use in such a market. Some of these practices can actually be dangerous in terms of later setting yourself up for a lawsuit. So make sure that you have a very well qualified Realtor® assisting you!) If disclosures and inspections are available before offers are presented to the seller, buyers may have reviewed and approved them upfront and may submit the signed copies of some or all of them along with the agency disclosure, offer, copy of the deposit check, and pre-approval letter from their lender. A strong seller's market will make the process of reviewing offers a little different than in a normal market; ask your agent what to expect ahead of time.

As the seller, you have the final determination whether or not to accept an offer. In the best of worlds, you will find a buyer who has enough money, is highly qualified and is very interested in your home. But in reality, there are often good buyers who may be first-time homebuyers, who are getting a low down payment or nothing-down loan, or are borrowing the earnest money to submit with the offer. We have submitted offers for first-time homebuyers with a promissory note as the earnest money. This is when the buyer promises to bring the money to closing, sometimes out of loan proceeds. We have also submitted offers with minimal earnest money; usually 1 percent of the purchase price is about the least acceptable deposit. It is then incumbent on your Realtor® to determine whether minimal earnest money should be a deterrent to the buyer's ability to purchase your home.

The buyer's agent may want to include one or more "extra" clauses in the offer to purchase to cover special requests. For example, they may want to have the carpet professionally steam cleaned prior to closing, and such a clause could be included in the contract. If the buyer is purchasing land on which to build a home, they would probably want to know if a survey, soil tests, or other information is available. Again, a clause would be inserted to cover that need. There are so many clauses, and so many special requests by buyers, that to cover them all would be impossible. You, as the seller, can insert your own clauses as well, with the help of your Realtor®, of course. One of our most common clauses states that the seller has the right to rent back the property after the close of escrow. This clause might be important for sellers when they have not yet found a new home.

Assuming you are presented with just one offer (although during a hot market, multiple offers are not uncommon), there are three possible responses: (1) you can accept the offer as submitted and sign it, officially accepting the offer; (2) you can reject the offer and hope they come back with a higher one or that another buyer will come along; or (3) you can counter the offer to modify its terms and conditions.

Once you have accepted the offer without question, do not try to second-guess the process. It is not the time to worry if you accepted too little or gave up too much. If you've done your homework, and you got what you wanted in the transaction, be happy. If the offer meets your needs, it may not be worthwhile trying to squeeze more out of it.

You should always respond to a legitimate offer. Hopefully your Realtor® will not let you ignore a good one. Recently, one of Ken's sellers had a property on the market at $799,000 and an offer came in at $719,000. She reacted to the offer as though it was insulting and would not even respond—this from a woman who regularly made very low offers on properties when she was the buyer. Ken told her that ignoring the offer was not an option; she hired him to sell her property and part of his responsibility was to communicate with every potential buyer until they either bought the property or went away. She said, "Fine, then tell them I'm holding out for full price." He did. Within an hour, the same buyer submitted a new offer at $785,000, and the seller accepted. There are, however, agents who forget their objectivity, become emotionally involved and take offers personally. When reviewing a buyer's low offer, we've had listing agents tell us, with all the resentment they can muster, "This is an insult. My seller won't even respond to this." The agent should realize that they are not the seller, *you* are. If there is a viable buyer who wants the property and is capable of buying it, they will run the risk of losing a sale for you.

Finally, although most rejected first offers elicit a counterproposal from the buyer you should beware. Often the first offer is the best and only offer. The negotiating process continues until you and the buyers have come to an agreement on the price, terms, inclusions, and exclusions which work for both of you. If the agents and their clients have done their work responsibly, it should be a transaction that makes everyone satisfied, even happy. It will be a win/win situation for everyone.

When you have agreed to all contents of the offer, everything is signed immediately. It's not a binding contract until everything is signed and the signature of acceptance is conveyed to the other side. A contract is simply an agreement between two or more people (called *parties*) to do certain things, and some form of exchange is made. In this case, when you and the buyer do what you have agreed to do in the contract, the deed to the house will be transferred to the buyer and you will get the money.

So now that you have a fully ratified contract, you are "in escrow." Your agent should provide you with a timeline (it is good to provide it to the other agent as well, so that everyone is basing their expectations on the same timeline) so that you know what is going to happen, and when.

Some of Your Responsibilities Are:

(1) transfer Disclosure Statement (required by law in most cases),

(2) supplemental Seller's Disclosure,

(3) lead Paint Disclosure for pre-1978 housing,

(4) natural Hazard Report,

(5) environmental Hazard Report,

(6)   other disclosures as required by the contract or suggested by your Realtor®, such as the Megan's Law disclosure, smoke, water heater, FRPTA, an insurance claims history disclosure, the C.L.U.E. report and so forth,

(7)   any inspections you've had done on the property,

(8)   a Preliminary Title Report, and

(9)   if applicable, CC&Rs (Covenants, Codes, and Restrictions), Association Bylaws, and any required condominium documents such as association minutes, financial statements, and reserves.

- letting the buyer and certain other people have access to the home for purposes of conducting any inspections, an appraisal, taking measurements, and so forth (you may feel invaded the first two weeks or so, and it is often easier to leave your home when they are there measuring, inspecting, and so forth);

- answering the buyer's legitimate questions about the house. Tip: Always ask for questions in writing, and respond in writing, as well. A paper-trail is important for your protection;

- showing up at the appointed time to sign the documents to transfer title of the property to the buyer. This is usually done at a title company;

- providing your loan payoff information to the title company;

- providing access to your home for needed repairs;

- having repairs done prior to close of escrow (unless otherwise agreed to in writing);

- contacting utility companies to transfer services to the buyer on the day of closing;

- being available for the final walk-through to answer questions about the house and how its various systems, such as the sprinklers and furnace, operate.

Some of the Buyer's Responsibilities Are:

- applying for a loan, if they haven't done this already, and providing all the information required by the lender to process that loan;

- getting the money necessary to close the purchase—down payment and closing costs;

- providing, and usually paying for, an appraisal to determine the current market value of the property (this is separate from the appraisal that you may have paid for yourself, earlier in the process, to determine the best selling price for your home);

- conducting any inspections of the property, usually with the help of a professional home inspector or other specialists (roofing, chimney, septic, pool, foundation, pest, soils, drainage, and so on);

- reviewing the disclosures and title and other documents provided by the title company and determining if they are acceptable;

- securing homeowner's insurance (it is advisable to do this right away);

- conducting a final walk-through of the house;

- deciding which lender and loan program they want prior to being in contract to purchase a home. Buyers are advised *not* to switch loan programs or lenders in the middle of escrow as this could cause delays to the escrow and can be considered as buyer's default; and

- showing up at the appointed time to sign escrow instructions, loan documents and deliver a cashier's check, or have money wired to the title company a day prior to the close of escrow.

Contingencies

Nearly every contract has contingencies which give one party the right to cancel the contract if certain things about the property are deemed unsatisfactory, or certain obligations are not met. For example, the loan contingency clause requires the buyer to apply for a loan by a certain date and to get the loan approval by another specific date. If the buyer's lender anticipates problems obtaining loan approval, it will be up to the buyer to cancel the contract by the loan approval deadline. In that event, the property will go back on the market. This is why it is so important the buyer be pre-approved. You don't want to re-list your home after it has lost the sizzle of being new on the market. The buyer has the right to review the title and association documents, and if the buyer finds those documents unacceptable, they can and may cancel the contract. Let's look at some of the major contingencies included in nearly every home purchase contract:

- The buyer normally has the right to conduct an inspection of your home in order to determine its condition, and that of everything included in the sale. This contingency gives the buyer the right to ask you to remedy things that may reduce the value of the home, and to terminate the contract if you can't reach an agreement on payment for potential repairs. This is why most professional Realtors® will recommend you obtain an inspection upfront and disclose the property condition to the buyer so that you are not held hostage when they conduct their own inspection. The buyer has the right to conduct their own inspections and are encouraged to do so. What's revealed from *their* inspection should not be radically different from what was revealed by the professionals *you* chose.

- Other contingencies can also be built into an offer, the inclusion of which will depend on a variety of circumstances. For example, perhaps the buyer must sell their current home before they will have the money to purchase your home (a Contingency for Sale or Purchase of Other Property—COP). In this case, they will want a contingency stating that if they cannot sell their existing home, they can terminate your purchase agreement. If you are willing to accept such a contingency, you should use it as a bargaining tool—maybe in exchange for a higher price or taking the home in "as-is" condition. In either case, you should always impose a definite time limit for the buyer to perform and you should also have the right to terminate the purchase agreement if they don't perform. This termination will allow you to put your property back on the market without any liability or obligation to the buyer.

- Another option is to insert a provision that will allow you to continue to market your property for sale while the buyer is trying to sell their property. This is accomplished by the inclusion of a "contingent sale-release clause." In the event the seller ac-

114

cepts another written purchase agreement from a subsequent buyer, the seller shall give written notice to the existing buyer that requires the buyer to remove the sale contingency in writing and provide documentation of sufficient funds and income to complete the sale of your home without first selling their home. If the buyer fails to remove this contingency within a specified time-frame, usually 72 hours from their receipt of the notice to do so, the seller may immediately cancel the agreement in writing. This contingent sale-release clause will allow you to keep the property on the market and hopefully attract a different buyer without a contingency to sell another property. But it's important to know that most agents won't show the home if it has an accepted offer or listed in the MLS as a contingent sale.

Inspection

In general, we always recommend that buyers obtain a professional home inspection on any property they buy. Just because a home is new doesn't mean that it is well built! In fact, many recently built condos often have inspections done and lawsuits filed before the statute of limitations passes. The buyer and their Realtor® should review the condominium documents to determine the responsibilities of the homeowners' association. For example, if heat is included in the dues, the association is generally responsible for maintaining heating systems. It is also generally responsible for outside maintenance, including painting, roof replacement, maintenance of common facilities such as a pool or clubhouse and so on. But if the heating system is separate for each condominium and the individual homeowners are responsible, the buyer must be able to also inspect the heating system if they want to. A buyer should use a professional for all inspections.

A good home inspector has been trained in all the systems and details that make up a house. A good home inspection will take from a couple of hours to a half day, depending on the size and complexity of your house. Make sure the buyers know about important positive facts, such as a newly replaced roof, rather than letting an inspector guess that it is five or six years old. Inspectors are not perfect, and the reality is that their inspections are mostly based on visual perceptions.

At the completion of the inspection, the inspector may take the buyer and their agent through the home to identify what might need attention. Those are things the buyer and their agent may want to discuss with you and your Realtor®. The buyer may ask you to remedy some or all of those items. Hopefully, the buyer's agent will inform them not to "sweat the small stuff." For example, if all the buyer finds in the home inspection are a bathtub or two that need caulking, furnace filters that need changing, an outside door that needs a new weather seal or some other minor detail, the buyer should agree to do the repairs themselves once they move in. However, occasionally the inspector will discover a condition that requires a specialist. For example, they may find a cracked or substandard foundation. In that case, they might recommend the buyer have a structural engineer inspect the foundation. Other serious issues, from the chimney to the furnace, may require different specialists.

Depending on the nature of the market, most buyers will request that you correct any major problems. If the heat exchanger on the furnace has a leak, it must be replaced, which can be costly. If any appliances do not work, the buyer may ask that they be repaired or replaced. If the roof is in such disrepair, or so old that replacement is imminent, the buyer may ask you to have it replaced prior to completing the sale. It is important to recognize that a serious issue will not simply go away and that regardless of the buyer, these types of concerns will ultimately need to be addressed.

When the buyer makes these requests, you can respond in a variety of ways: you can agree to have the problems remedied prior to closing if you think that the cost to you is reasonable in relation to the sales price; you can refuse on the grounds that the price the buyer negotiated on the house does not leave you enough money to make the corrections; or you may offer to settle with the buyer somewhere in between. If you do not have the cash to fix the furnace, for example, but recognize that it needs repairing, you can offer to compensate the buyer at closing and let the buyer have it repaired after the home is theirs. As long as you and the buyer can resolve the inspection items to your mutual satisfaction, and you put the agreement in writing, you can proceed to closing. If you cannot resolve the issues, the buyer can cancel the contract and move on. In fact, if the buyer finds a serious, ongoing problem (like the foundation wall), the buyer may want to terminate the offer outright.

And even if the buyer asks for minor items to be addressed, you should seriously consider whether you are willing to lose the contract rather than address the items. Sometimes, half a day with a handyman can make everyone happy. On the other hand, we've had more than one seller for whom we negotiated one or more back-up offers, sometimes for more than the original contract. So, the seller was able to refuse all inspection requests, knowing he had other buyers waiting in line. It is important to point out that per contract, the inspections and reports that the buyer generates become material fact for subsequent buyers. The seller will need to disclose these new deficiencies no matter who the next buyer is. Example: if the first buyer's inspection reveals a cracked chimney and if for any reason this sale doesn't not go through, the seller must now disclose to future potential buyers the crack in the chimney. To give the buyer a chance to inspect to their hearts content, the seller should make sure that they are *not* there when the inspector goes through.

Title Documents and Easements

The contract will describe a certain document that you are obligated to provide to the buyer called a Preliminary Title Report. It is a legal picture of the title to the property. It shows who owns the property (hopefully, you), the existing lender, the initial amount of your loan, and any easements or restrictions which convey with the property. Also, it shows other things about the property that need to be cleared up prior to closing or which might impede the buyer's ability to purchase the home.

The buyer and their agent will review these documents in order to ensure there are no title problems that would prevent the buyer from getting clear title to the property. For example, if there are liens or obligations against the property which total more than the purchase price, the buyer should immediately inquire as to how those debts are going to be paid. Typically, with the exceptions of most recorded easements or deed restrictions, buyers do not want to take title of a property that has obligations against it which cannot be cleared by the title company at closing. It might be that some of the obligations shown in the title documents have actually been paid, but the payments have not been recorded with the county clerk. A simple recording of the documents would clear those debts.

Some problems disclosed in a title search may be very simple to remedy. For example, if the title is shown to be held in the names of both a husband and wife as joint tenants, but one has died, a simple recording of the death certificate will remove that person from the title, enabling the surviving spouse to transfer title to the buyer.

There are also things on virtually every set of title documents that will remain with the property even after sale. Utility companies that have power, sewer, water, and cable lines running to the property will generally have a continuing easement to go onto the land for purposes of repair, replacement, or installation of utilities. This is limited to the areas designated on the parcel map.

An easement is not an actual title to or ownership of property. It is simply a recorded agreement giving access to another person or entity for limited purposes. Local governments might have easements for a variety of reasons, such as access to power poles. For instance, some beach communities allow public access to the water. An easement may give a neighbor the right to cross your property to get to their own, or to share a driveway if they are otherwise unable to get reasonable access to their home. Easements are very common and should not deter a buyer from purchasing your home. If they have an experienced Realtor®, they should already be informed of this fact.

Common Interest Communities—Neighborhood and Condo Associations

In the 1960s, neighborhoods were established and communities grew without a lot of community planning. In older cities, you will often find that homes in the same neighborhood can be very different from one another—a craftsman next to a mid century (50s) tract. Sometimes, commercial, residential, and industrial buildings are randomly interspersed. Over time, governing authorities (town councils and county governments) have usually developed rules and regulations that give them the authority to approve what is built, to ensure that some consistency exists in each neighborhood development and to designate how homes, stores, and industrial development will be separated.

Restrictions on building, imposed by both governments and developers, have flourished in the past 50 years, but for different reasons. Governments want to control growth and developers want to preserve values.

Therefore, depending on the neighborhood, the developer may have filed documents with the governing authority that establish certain guidelines. These are generally known as the *covenants, conditions, and restrictions* (CC&Rs) for a neighborhood. These documents often incorporate a set of architectural guidelines, which may be more or less restrictive than local building codes.

If you are selling a condominium or townhouse, the documents are called the declaration and bylaws. Because this type of property is typically managed by a homeowners' association there will also be a set of rules and regulations. The association collects dues, the amount of which it adjusts from time to time, and will have a set of financial documents showing how well it has managed the condominium complex. Alternately, some attached properties such as duplexes or town homes may have only a homeowner's association agreement and rules and regulations. This distinction occurs when those properties have an underlying lot as opposed to strictly common grounds or limited common elements.

All of these documents should be provided to the buyer along with the title documents. If they are not, have your Realtor® determine if such documents exist, and if so, have them get copies for the buyer. It is important for the buyer to review them, and a provision for this will likely be included in your contract for sale. The restrictions imposed by these documents may be perfectly acceptable to the buyer. For example, some neighborhood associations will not allow anyone to have junk cars parked in front of homes and will not allow the buyer to conduct auto repairs on the property. If the buyer happens to be a backyard mechanic, this type of neighborhood may not be suitable for them.

Some associations restrict the size and number of household pets. Some condominium associations insist that anything stored on a deck (like bicycles) not be visible from the street. These restrictions and requirements should be reviewed by the buyer during the title review period. For example, an RV owner would be unpleasantly surprised to find out after closing that the covenants prohibited RVs from being parked anywhere on the property. Restrictions are to be expected when buying a condo or a house in a planned community, this should not affect the sale.

If you are selling a condominium, townhouse or other property that requires the payment of dues and assessments, you are required to provide the buyer with the HOA's financial statements, copies of the minutes of the past twelve months' board of directors meetings, and the budget and financial statements to help them determine whether the HOA is financially viable—if it has established reserves to cover major periodic maintenance such as roofs, paved parking areas, and painting. If reserves are not substantial enough, homeowners could be faced with future special assessments where every homeowner is asked to pay a set amount (sometimes totaling thousands of dollars), to pay for a needed improvement to the whole complex. If the buyer reviews the minutes or places a telephone call to a member of the association's board of directors, they can also get information about what the association is planning. By doing this, the buyer will also get a feel for the "politics" of the board—whether there are one or more members who consider it their personal fiefdom.

These are all things that should be disclosed to the buyer in the title and association documents. The buyer will have an opportunity to review these documents, and it is important for them to voice any objections before the stated deadline. If there is anything they cannot live with, they have the right to terminate the contract within a reasonable period of time (usually designated within the purchase contract).

The Appraisal

If the buyer is having part of the purchase financed with a loan, the loan will generally be contingent on a lender receiving a satisfactory appraisal of value. The buyer has the option of including an appraisal contingency even if they are paying cash.

An appraisal is a process whereby a licensed professional examines your home, reviews similar properties that have been sold recently and gives an opinion of the fair-market value of your property. However, at this phase, the appraiser also looks at the contract in place between you and the buyer. If they determine that the contract sets a price that is fairly close to the value established by looking at comparable sold properties, they will likely establish a fair-market value at, or close to, your contract price.

If your contract price is substantially different, then the fair-market value may be either higher or lower. If the appraisal is higher than what you have agreed to sell the home for, you should not be too concerned, especially if you did your homework. If it comes in lower (even by $1), and you have allowed the buyer to make the appraisal a contingency in the contract, they have the right to terminate the contract. The contract can be kept intact, however, by one of three agreements: (1) they agree to a larger down payment (because their lender will only lend based on the appraised value); (2) you agree to lower the contract price; or (3) you and the buyers agree to settle some place in between.

financing

In most states, the buyer may lose their earnest money deposit if they default on the contract, plus additional penalties could be imposed. If they are financing the purchase, they will usually request a contingency for such a case. In other words, the buyer would be given a certain amount of time for the lender to approve their loan within established parameters. In some states, if the buyer does not have full loan approval at terms acceptable to them by the loan approval deadline, they must provide you with written notice to terminate the contract.

If the buyer is having difficulty getting the loan they want and a lender suggests another loan that will work, you and your agent may want to negotiate a limited extension of the contract. Whether you agree to cooperate will depend on how interested you are in continuing to work with the buyer. If the buyer does not terminate the contract under a loan contingency, and subsequently fails to qualify for a loan and cannot continue with the purchase, they are considered in default.

It is critically important that you and your Realtor® be cognizant of all contract deadlines and who must perform what obligations by each deadline. Then you will be able to protect your rights under the contract, including your right to earnest money if the contract is wrongfully terminated.

9. Preparing for Uncle Sam

In preparing for the sale of our house, Samia lined up some key resources for us—a fantastic interior designer to help with the staging of the house, several inspection services, and an extremely competent escrow agent. She creatively marketed our house by setting up a website with a URL in the name of our address, listings in the MLS, and designing colorful brochures. We received an offer very soon after we listed the house. During the escrow period, Samia was also extremely attentive to the details of the closing and worked tirelessly to keep things on track. We are in the process of tearing down and building a new house and our contractor is yet again another excellent referral from Samia.

—Côme Laguë and Charlene Li

Whether you're self-employed, a wage earner, or have your own business, you know that Uncle Sam, through the Internal Revenue Service, is your silent partner. It's no different when you sell your home. When you sell it for more than you paid, you create a taxable gain. However, just as you were able to take deductions on your tax return for the interest you paid while living in your home, Uncle Sam has created some wonderful tax benefits when you sell your home.

Please be aware that we are *not* providing tax advice. As we said in the beginning of this book, we really have tried to be as accurate as possible when it comes to what works and what doesn't in selling a home. In this section, we will talk about how the tax laws work in your favor as a home seller. We have attempted to ensure that everything said here is accurate and relevant, but laws change, circumstances vary and there is always the possibility for error. Using the guidance offered here, along with your selection of a competent tax professional, whether a Certified Public Accountant or a tax attorney, you should feel confident in selling real estate and legally avoiding taxes on any gain you may have created. We always recommend you consult with your tax advisor before making any financial decisions.

Primary Home Rollover

Let's start with the first tax advantage: In the past, if you sold your home and purchased another, all the gain from the appreciation in the value of your old home could be transferred to your new one without owing current income or capital gains taxes, provided you rolled that gain over into a new home within 24 months of selling your old one. This was under IRS Code Section 1034, prior to the Taxpayer Relief Act (TRA) of 1997. Section 1034 also replaced IRS Code Section 121, which was designed for taxpayers who were over age 55 and allowed a $500,000 exclusion for married couples or a $250,000 exclusion for a single person on the sale of their principal residence. Now you no longer need to buy another house of equal or greater value to claim the exclusion.

You can take advantage of the new law over and over again (even before age 55, although not more than once every two years), but there are certain guidelines. First, the property must be your principal residence and not a second home or rental property. Second, it may be a detached house, a mobile home, a co-op apartment or a condominium, but you cannot have more than one principal residence at the same time. Third, you must have lived in the house for at least two of the last five years prior to the sale, but they don't have to be continuous— you could live in the home for more than six months for four different years and that could work too. Check with your tax advisor. There is even a benefit to a spouse who is not living in the house at the time of the sale; they can claim up to $250,000 of tax-free profits, provided they too lived in the home for two of the last five years. This also applies to two co-owners who are not married, as long as they meet the occupancy rules.

Even if one spouse dies, these tax benefits are available. The surviving spouse, whether widow or widower, is allowed to claim the full $500,000 exclusion if the home is sold in the same year that the spouse died.

Section 1034 eliminates most of the record-keeping requirements if you know that your gain will be less than $250,000. By the way, the gain you are allowed to exclude is the lesser of your gain up to $250,000. In other words, if your gain is $100,000 on the sale of your home, you do not get to take a $250,000 deduction. Your escrow company has to file a Form 1099-S and report your taxable gain to the IRS. However, if you take a loss on the sale of your home, you can't deduct that loss; remember, you had been getting an interest deduction.

Investment Property Exchanges

Tax deferral is also available when you sell a rental home or an apartment building if you follow the guidelines in IRS Code Section 1031. This is called a *1031 tax-deferred exchange,* and is a powerful way to create wealth through real estate. You can sell investment property and transfer all of the gain to another, larger investment property and defer the taxes that would have been due on a straight sale.

Here's how it works: An investor/taxpayer can defer the taxes on the sale of investment property and qualify for *exchange* treatment if the property was held as investment property, or for use in a trade or business, and was exchanged from property that was like that which was sold. This is called *like-kind.* However, prior to the sale of the old property the seller must enter into an exchange agreement with a *qualified intermediary.* This person or company structures the exchange transaction to meet all of the IRS Code requirements.

What Is a Qualified Intermediary?

A qualified intermediary is also known as a *facilitator* or *accommodator.* This is a person, or company, who holds the funds from your sale and structures the transaction to meet IRS requirements. Unfortunately, there are no federal or state laws that govern an accommodator. Anyone can claim to qualify; however, it cannot be anyone close to you, or who takes instructions from you: such as your accountant, attorney, banker, employee, real estate professional, or family member. You must confirm that they are qualified, that they have the knowledge, experience and credentials to perform for you. Also, since they will hold your money, you want to be sure they don't take an extended trip to a country without an extradition treaty with the United States.

Ask the accommodator if they pay interest on your funds. Ask for their fee structure and whether there are extra charges if you require additional consultations. Verify that they are members of the national organization for qualified intermediaries, the Federation of Exchange Accommodators (FEA). Confirm that they carry an independent bond issued by an insurance company that specializes in this type of coverage. This is one of the most important items. You don't want to be left empty-handed if your money is stolen by the intermediary or one of their employees.

IRS Guidelines

There are three basic guidelines set out by the IRS to qualify for exchange treatment. First, the purchase price of the replacement property must be equal to, or greater than, the property you sold.

Second, the debt on the replacement property, the loan, must be equal to, or greater than, the debt held on the property you sold. There should be no relief of your debt.

Third, all of the net proceeds, the total amount you received for your property, must be used to buy the replacement property.

If you don't follow these three guidelines, you can still complete the exchange, but you may have taxes to pay. As an example, if you hold out $100,000 from the exchange (this is called *boot*), it will be taxed. When attempting a partial exchange it is crucial you get competent tax advice.

Like-Kind Property

Like-kind refers to the type of property involved in an exchange. According to the IRS, this is "any property held for productive use in a trade or business or held for investment purposes." As an example, you can exchange an apartment building for a commercial building, or a rental single-family home for an apartment building or a shopping center. Even raw or vacant land and a leasehold for 30 years or more count under exchange rules.

The following property is not considered real estate, and therefore does not count as exchange property: money, stocks, bonds and notes. Also, limited partnerships and your primary residence do not qualify.

Time Frame

Most exchanges occur as delayed exchanges, and there are two key deadlines to keep in mind. The first is the 45-day period to identify the property you want to acquire after the close of escrow on your property. The second is the 180-day period by which you must close escrow on your replacement property. There are no exceptions or extensions. There is a special factor which few people know about—if the 180 day period ends after the day your taxes are due, be sure to file an extension to file your taxes!

You have two choices when it comes to identifying your replacement property. The first is the *three-property rule,* and the second is the *200 percent rule.* The three-property rule allows you to identify up to three properties that you want to acquire as an exchange. You may purchase one or all of the properties to complete your exchange as long as they follow the IRS guidelines described earlier. If you choose to purchase more than three properties, you must qualify under the 200 percent rule, which allows you to identify as many properties as you want as long as the total market value of all the identified properties is less than 200 percent of the value of the sold property. You will need to complete an *identification notice* for your qualified intermediary to comply with the IRS rules.

Most often, when sellers consider a tax-deferred exchange they are dealing with large amounts of money. Competent advice is suggested because the penalty for failure to follow the rules is substantial. Please consult qualified professionals.

Section II

Buying Your Next Home

Buying Your Next Home

Ira and Carol Serkes represented us when we bought our first home in Oakland. They took the time to explain things to us patiently and thoroughly and gave us great advice at every step of the process. With their help, we were able to write a winning purchase offer in a seller's market. When we decided to move to another town and needed to sell our first home quickly, we trusted the Serkes to be up to the challenge. They made some great suggestions for staging the house for sale and gave it prime placement on Realtor.com. Every suggestion Ira and Carol made turned out to be exactly right. What was especially great for us is that the Serkes' understand how to leverage technology for marketing properties as well as for communicating with their clients. Potential buyers really appreciated the great digital images of our house and the neighborhood that the Serkes' included with the listing on their website. If you ever want to buy or sell a house in Berkeley, North Oakland, Albany, El Cerrito, or anything nearby, you won't regret working with Ira and Carol Serkes.

—Aviva Rosenstein and Noah Friedman

It is sometimes difficult to balance selling your home while trying to buy a new home. The timing is often hard to gauge. Should you wait until you have a contract before you start looking? And if you wait too long, could you face a period of "homelessness?" Don't panic. Like all other aspects of buying and selling real estate, planning is everything. Make a backup plan for what you will do if your present house is sold before you find a new one. Or conversely, make a plan for how you will deal with the possibility of owning two homes for a period of time. Your choices should depend on your time frame and your budget.

The strategy you take for buying a new home depends upon the market conditions. In a strong seller's market, when there is a lot of competition for homes on the market, we recommend getting a bridge (or swing) loan on your current home so you can make an offer which isn't contingent upon first selling your home. Once you finish your inspection contingency on the new home, put your home on the market. Ira has been particularly effective coordinating the two transactions so that his clients don't own two homes at the same time for more than a few days.

In a strong buyer's market, you may be better off waiting until your home has an offer accepted, and the inspection contingencies have been removed, before searching for a new home.

In either case, try to negotiate a long escrow, or rent back, so that you're not homeless!

Another option is to rent your house until it sells, but we don't recommend that for several reasons. Houses with renters are generally harder to sell. Renters take worse care of a home, so it never "shows" as well, and buyers are reluctant to deal with the possibility of having to evict someone if the tenant refuses to leave after the sale. Because potential "double moves" are expensive, you can put your belongings in storage and stay with friends or relatives, or try to lease back your sold house for a short period of time. This is commonly done. Be sure to put a leaseback clause into the contract if you are considering this option. The seller can sometimes lease back for up to 60 days while paying the buyer on a per day basis. Unlike a regular lease, where a renter pays a monthly fee, in this case the seller would pay the daily cost of the buyer's principal, interest, taxes, and insurance (PITI). In a hot seller's market, it's not uncommon for the buyers to offer the seller a free leaseback for 30 to 60 days! Whenever Ira knows that his seller would like to stay in the house after close of escrow, he always informs the buyer before they write their offer. Ask, and you receive! And, of course, you can always rent some form of short-term housing. Since your Realtor® knows your needs best, they can often be a very good source for finding affordable short-term housing, especially if you have children or pets. Planning ahead should include familiarizing yourself with types of homes, neighborhoods, and areas of interest so that you will be prepared to move quickly once your home is under contract.

Another rule of thumb to follow is to buy first when prices are heading up, and sell first when they are heading down. That way you are in the best position to do well in the market. Like we've said before, planning is the key to making a smooth purchase, or sale of property.

10. Play the Field and Lose the Game

Anytime I needed something, it was provided. Everything went according to the plan that Pete and his team had developed for us. Timing was very important to us since we were buying and selling at the same time. Pete did everything to make sure that the close of escrows were close together. Lo and behold, there was only 10 days between the two.

—Ed and Maria Villanueva, Pleasant Hill

If you had a good experience with your agent in the sale, you would want to use the same person to help you buy your new home. Not all Realtors® represent both buyers and sellers, but it's always a good place to start, especially if you are moving within the same area.

If you are working with one Realtor® who knows you won't hop around from one to the next, they will become as committed to you as you are to them. They will become "your" Realtor®, and they will be working for you. They will likely work to help you get qualified for financing, and when that "hot" property comes on the market, guess who they're going to call? Believe us, it won't be the person who happened to call in on an ad; it will be you—the buyer to whom they are committed. After all, you are giving them a substantial amount of business and they will want to bring to your attention any property they can find that fits your needs.

We've sold numerous properties where our buyer was the only person to see the house. We try to check new listings regularly and also watch the newspaper classifieds for homes being sold by owners. Sometimes we see a property that is obviously underpriced, or perhaps "priced for a quick sale." It then becomes imperative to get our buyer into the property before anyone else sees it because we know it will go fast. We're off with a quick call to the buyer to let them know, "We've got one." We can usually write an offer to purchase or a contract that same day. We know the timing of your sale and we know when you need to find that new home. You will find that two-way loyalty pays off. The key is selecting the right agent.

But what if you are moving to a new area and need to find a home? Obviously, you'll need to find someone who can represent your interests as a buyer. We belong to extraordinary networks of excellent Realtors® across the United States and Canada. Just send us an email or give us a call and we will refer you so someone who will take superb care of you, ideally a real estate agent who holds the ABR (Accredited Buyer Representation) professional designation.

Usually when you enlist the services of a buyer's agent, you will be working with a Realtor® who will represent your interests as a sort of personal representative. This is known as an agency relationship.

Agency

When you work with a buyer's agent, you will often enter into a representation contract. A buyer broker contract is a contract between the buyer (you) and the Realtor®, and it works two ways. First, the Realtor® becomes your agent and is obligated to represent your best interests. Second, the contract represents your commitment to the Realtor® and says that you will work exclusively with them. This agreement means that when you see a sign on a property, you will not call the listing agent yourself to negotiate the transaction, nor will you go into a property that is for-sale-by-owner to do the same. Instead, you will call your agent and ask them to get you information on the property. You now have an agent; use them. The whole purpose of this exercise is to get you a home with the best terms and conditions. If you have selected a good agent, you should recognize that they have the experience and the skills necessary to represent you effectively.

There are a few items you should pay particular attention to in a buyer-agency contract. In some states, most are already part of the standard contract, but elsewhere, this may not be the case. Before you sign, at least discuss the following topics.

Confidentiality

If you are to be represented effectively, it is imperative that the agent keeps any information they learn about you confidential. In particular, your financial situation, willingness to accept concessions, and motivating factors for the purchase should not be revealed, except as a valid negotiating tool and with your prior consent.

In addition, you have a right to be assured that confidential information remains confidential even after you have bought your home or after your contract with the agent has expired or been terminated in any way. If you make an offer on an in-house transaction (where the seller is also represented by the brokerage representing you), your information should remain just as confidential as when negotiating for a property listed by another firm.

Scope of Work

The contract will contain a description of what type of property your agent is instructed to seek for you. Make sure the description fits your needs. If you are looking specifically for a residence, make sure that the language limits the search to just that. Do not accept language that says "any property." If you are considering purchasing a home from a family member or friend, you may ask to have that property excluded from the contract; however, you may want to ask your agent what they would charge to handle that transaction for you. Pitfalls can still exist, and in fact can be more serious and more heart-wrenching when dealing with someone close to you. Many close relationships have been damaged or ruined when friends and relatives have done business together. It's usually not because of a lack of good intentions, but when objectivity is lost, personal feelings get exaggerated and hurt, eroding the process. We've worked on numerous transactions where family members and close friends were involved, and we have found that it becomes vitally important to ensure a win/win situation for everyone involved.

Many buyer agents typically write contracts for six months, which may or may not be a long time depending on your availability and the type of market in which you are buying, i.e seller's or buyer's market. We often work with buyers relocating from other areas or buyers of second homes, and the process involves communicating while they are in another city or state. We will coordinate property showings to coincide with trips to the area, and sometimes they buy properties we've recommended sight unseen. Even when working with locals, using a six-month representation period makes sense.

This long period can be scary. What if you decide you don't like your agent? What if your plans change? The simplest answer is to ask for a cancellation clause. Always include a clause that says that either party, the buyer or agent, may cancel the contract for any reason whatsoever, by providing written notice to the other party. While they may ask for ten-day advance notice, people who are not compatible should not have to work together. If your Realtor® is willing to give you this "out" in your contract, you can bet they are confident in their ability to represent you effectively. Keep in mind that you are not able to cancel a contract for a property on which you are already negotiating, and every contract will have what is called a "holdover" clause that entitles your agent to a commission if, after your contract has terminated, you buy a property the agent showed you.

The entire contract should be designed to be fair to both parties. It is fair to be able to cancel a contract when two people cannot work together. It is not fair to have someone do a lot of work for you and then you cancel. You should be able to determine in the first or second meeting with your Realtor® whether or not you are compatible. Don't spend several weeks or months together and then decide to go with someone else.

Again, if you do the same research to find a buyer's agent as you did to find your seller's agent, you should have the right person to help you find your next home (refer to the credentials mentioned in Chapter 2). If you are moving within the same area and can rely on the relationship with your present Realtor®, you are in a great position, but make sure your Realtor® will sign a Buyer Brokerage contract with you.

11. Lender Contracts

Ira and Carol, Gayle and I would like to thank you for all the great work you did in marketing our home and the remarkable price you brought in. It was an absolute stroke of luck and a real pleasure for us to put ourselves in the hands of such true professionals. We had lived in our home in Albany for over twenty-seven years and we were apprehensive that putting it up for sale would be a trying and difficult process. Quite the contrary. You kept us informed and updated throughout the process. I want you to know that we both regard you as being truly sincere and fine people!

—Harry & Gayle Willett

Real estate is a truly great investment! There is probably nowhere else where you can leverage so much with so little. You can purchase a $800,000 home with $40,000. If that home goes up in value $80,000 (or 10 percent) in a year, you've doubled your $40,000 investment (100 percent). Sound too good to be true? It's not. People do it everyday. The best place to start investing in life is in your personal residence. If you are considering renting—don't do it! Renting is a losing proposition. All the money goes out and none comes back to you. As a homeowner, you get an appreciating asset and the tax advantage of deducting your property taxes and the interest portion of your payment. But for now, let's talk about how to get the majority of the money to buy your next home.

First, you need to find a lender. Make sure you have a lender that specializes in providing loans for the type of purchase you are making. If you are buying a home, you will use a residential lender, and if you are buying land, with certain exceptions, you will probably use a bank. A lender can do land loans if you are buying a lot and plan to build a home on it immediately. Many lenders now offer what is called a *one-time close, construction-to-perm* loan, which will help you finance the land purchase, provide the construction financing and then provide the permanent financing once the home is built.

Although we have already discussed lenders in regard to the sale of your home, once you are ready to buy, it is your turn to find financing with the best terms possible. Whether you use a loan officer at a bank, a broker, or a lender recommended by your Realtor®, you will want to make sure that they work hard to get you the best loan arrangement they can. At the end of the day, when you commit to a loan, the lender makes a commission. Make sure that they earn it!

In all states, banks are regulated by various government agencies in their practice of providing home loans. The state of California requires that lenders be licensed. It is important to be diligent in selecting your lender and loan officer; they can hold the key to your purchase.

A loan officer is much like a real estate agent: You may be referred to one by a friend, have a family member in the business, or happen to meet one by accident. Just remember that not all loan officers are alike. A good Realtor® will have a short list of lenders and loan officers who have proven that they know what they are doing, only make promises that they can keep, don't spring last-minute surprises on clients, have a substantial menu of loans to cover most situations and have competitive rates and costs. You want to avoid last-minute surprises, such as discovering that the underwriter has a list of conditions a day or two before you are supposed to close.

Beware of lenders who advertise low rates in major newspapers or on the Internet. Purchasers have often begun a loan application before meeting and retaining a quality Realtor® to assist in their home purchase. In many cases, where clients stayed with these lenders, they have later regretted their selection. Typically, something goes wrong. The most common problems are interest rate increases, disregarding good faith estimates, hidden fees, processing delays and lost documents.

A good Realtor® will also be familiar with the basics of loan processing and the types of loans available so that they can provide guidance as you work with the lender, and can tell if the person you are working with is knowledgeable. We feel teamwork will get more transactions done and we tend to stay out of it unless there's a problem and then we brainstorm unique possibilities with our buyers and their lenders.

A recent first-time homebuyer, whom we'll call Bob, started out with a lender Pete had recommended. Then Bob found a "great" rate on the Internet and chose to go with the Internet lender instead.

Remember our warning earlier? Bob decided he wanted to switch his loan to the lender who quoted the lowest rates. Clients always have the right to choose their own lenders, but we do caution them when we are not familiar with a lender they choose. We cannot vouch for that lender's service, competence, or knowledge. Often we interview a lender to determine the viability of the loan program they're offering, to get a sense of how well that lender can represent the client and to obtain a list of references to check.

Because Bob found his lender on the Internet, the lender was from another state and therefore was not familiar with local market customs. The lender was supposed to order the appraisal but never did, thinking that it was Bob's responsibility. Unfortunately, this was not discovered until the day before closing. The closing had to be postponed and, of course, by this time, Bob's rate lock had expired. But thanks to Pete's connections, he was able to get him a new loan through the original lender with a similar rate to the original loan and in the end everyone was happy.

A good faith estimate is a form your lender provides you with that shows the lender's regular charges, along with the other anticipated closing costs involved with the loan. It utilizes those figures to estimate the total amount of cash you will need in order to buy your house and calculates your approximate monthly payment. Some lenders will insist that they cannot provide a good faith estimate until you have a property under contract or in escrow. That's just not true. Good faith estimates are simply that—estimates—and they can be prepared quickly and easily. In fact, some lenders we work with will prepare several, one for each loan scenario you are considering. It assists you in comparing those loans so you can decide which one to take.

It also gives you something to compare with other lenders if you happen to be shopping for the best rates and costs. If one lender charges, for example, a $450 loan processing fee, and another charges $150, and the rates and other fees are the same, you might want to spend more time with the lender who charges less. But do not let these fees be the only reason for selecting a lender. Consider what happened to Bob. A good lender is worth their weight in gold.

You should also get a good faith estimate on two other occasions: (1) when you have a property under contract and your Realtor® provides a copy of that contract to the lender; and (2) when you change loan programs, either because you don't qualify for the one you started with, or you decide on a different plan. Once you are under contract, many of the items that were estimated on the first good faith estimate are known, so the estimate is more accurate and closer to reality.

Last-Minute Fees

Occasionally, one of our clients decides to use a lender we haven't recommended. In one case, a couple Ken represented decided to work with a lender who was renting a home from one of their parents. The lender promised to cut his origination fee in half because of the relationship. Usually, lenders charge a 1.0 percent loan origination fee. That fee is generally split between loan officers and the lender they work for. In this case, the lender either gave up his portion of that fee, or worked it out with his boss to discount the transaction. At any rate, when Ken compared his good faith estimate with those of other lenders, the reduced fee made the difference. Their loan was going to be about $580,000, so a 1.0 percent fee would have been $5,800. They could have saved a lot of money by going with this lender, all other things being equal.

Ken met with the lender and told him that if he really took care of the clients, he would get other referrals from him. The lender was just getting established in the area and was eager for the new business. However, it took him longer to process the loan than he said it would, and Ken did not have a settlement statement until the actual day of closing. Ken called both him and the title company to bring something to their attention—the fact that there was a 1.0 percent loan origination fee on the statement rather than 0.5 percent—and asked for a correction. But the loan officer insisted he had met with the clients, and because they had not locked in their rates and rates had gone up somewhat, he took a full origination fee rather than increase the rate.

Ken asked to see the new good faith estimate that he should have provided if this were true. He said he did not provide one, but the clients understood the new loan terms. The clients insisted there was no such agreement, and at the closing table they were faced with a dilemma. They had to close with the charges as they appeared, get the lender to write them a check for the 0.5 percent difference or walk away and refuse to close on the home. They closed, and did not get a refund from the lender. They were angry with him but happy to be in their new home. That lender has never received a referral from Ken, and within a few months he gone from the area. He certainly does not rent from the clients' parents anymore.

Loan Types and Interest Rates

There are a variety of loan types available and the loan program you select will depend first on your ability to qualify, and then on your right to select one over another.

A starting place regarding your ability to qualify for a loan is the quality of your credit report. Every lender uses the FICO score, which stands for the company that created the scoring formula: Fair Isaac Company. They are a third party that provides the score to a potential lender. The lender does not calculate the score, but uses it to establish a borrower's credit worthiness. Until recently, the components of this scoring system were kept secret, but it's been announced that consumers will be able to get information about their score at www.myFICO.com. In general, they use different models and adjust the score depending on various factors, such as the amount of credit, the level of credit cards with no balances, cards with high balances, bankruptcy, payment patterns and so on.

At the current time, a score over 700 is excellent. Scores of 620 or above would normally allow you to qualify for A or A+ quality loans. These have the lowest interest rates and the most favorable terms. If we hypothetically use interest rates of 7 percent as the best available, a person with a score over 620 would qualify for that rate. Scores below 620 would normally put you in what is called a "sub-prime" category, also called "B" or "C" loans. The interest rate would depend on a variety of information specific to your credit report, but is usually higher than the 7 percent A or A+ loans. The rules vary considerably between lenders on sub-prime loans.

In addition to the money the borrower would pay for doing a credit check, getting title insurance and paying escrow charges and appraisal fees, there is a cost to get most loans: *points*. Points refer to the cost of purchasing a loan. One point represents 1 percent of the loan balance. On a $600,000 loan this would be $6,000 to purchase the loan. If a credit score puts someone in the B or C range, the points could rise to 4, meaning it could cost up to $24,000 to purchase a loan. Other fees could rise from $450 to process the same paperwork for a typical A borrower, to $650 for a B or C borrower.

Certain loans are specially targeted for first-time homebuyers and offer features such as low down payment (as little as nothing down), competitive interest rates and the ability to have a cosigner or receive down payment assistance from another source. There are so many loan variables that it would be impossible to discuss them all here.

At the time of this writing, second-home loans are available with a 10 percent down payment and interest rates as low as on primary residences. Investment loans can be obtained for as little as 10 percent down (although 20 percent or more is most common), and the interest rates are somewhat higher. The more money you put down and the better qualified you are to repay the loan, the more likely the lender will be willing to give you the best terms and rates. Interest rates are around the lowest they have been in decades.

At this point, nearly anyone with decent credit and a job can buy a home. You can't always get exactly what you want the first time, but owning, saving, and taking advantage of a growing market may give you the ability to take your increased equity every couple of years and trade into a better home. And maybe you are someone who is doing just that.

Your Credit

As discussed above, in the past it was hard to be an informed consumer in the loan arena because much of the personal credit information used by lenders was unavailable to you. You couldn't find out either your credit score or the criteria used to develop that score. Consequently, consumers were unable to take proactive steps to improve their credit. Luckily, in the very recent past this has changed. The federal government has now passed a law that requires credit bureaus to release both your three-agency credit report score (FICO) and the bureaus' rating criteria upon requests from consumers. For a small fee you can now obtain this information or, as discussed previously, you can contact www.myFICO.com.

There are also credit repair agencies that work with consumers to raise their FICO scores. These agencies work with credit companies regularly, so they understand how to fix mistakes and how consumers can rearrange or repair their own credit, possibly raising their scores as much as 40 to 100 points. This process can even be as quick as a few short weeks for people who need quick credit fixes.

There are also many federal agencies designed to help homebuyers. They can help with home loans, credit counseling and even down-payment assistance. But beware of nonprofit credit counseling services. Although these services can consolidate debt for people who have trouble paying their bills, credit counseling is often looked at in the same light as bankruptcy when it comes to credit bureau scoring.

12. Loan Abuses

Just wanted to drop you a quick note saying how enjoyable it was working with you on the purchase of our new home. You made the entire experience a very exciting and enjoyable one. You have a great list of contacts from termite inspections to the cable company. Your expertise in the market conditions, coupled with your negotiating skills put us in to the house of our dreams, at a price we could afford. Thanks for everything.

—Mitch and Tammy Stewart, Nordstrom

Since buyers never really know the exact amount of their loan, or closing costs until they are at the closing table, there can be both the appearance, and the unfortunate reality of loan abuse. Although this has changed somewhat in the last few years due to both truth in lending statements, and the emergence of standardized closing costs, this is an area where you must make sure to protect yourself.

One reason for these recent changes is the current competitive market. A competitive market works to your advantage if you know how to make it work for you. First, regardless of your credit, in a competitive market it pays to shop around. Look for companies that offer a locked-in rate and standardized closing costs. This will help you avoid eleventh-hour changes.

By law you are entitled to a truth-in-lending disclosure that should give you a fairly accurate reflection of your loan payments and the closing costs. Although these are never completely accurate, they are a helpful reflection of the loan and fees associated with it.

As of this writing, if your loan is for less than $417,000 (approximately), it is considered a *conforming* loan and therefore, you can qualify for the best rates. If your credit is good, make sure you look for a conforming and not a *jumbo* loan (currently over $650,000) to get the best interest rates in this market. Jumbo loan rates are higher than conforming—these limits typically change from time to time so check with your lender for the current amounts.

Another way you can protect yourself is by not just knowing who your lender is, but by finding out ahead of time who will be servicing your loan. Servicing is frequently sold. Even though you pick a particular lender, after you sign the loan papers you may not have any control over the service. The "servicer" receives your payments, keeps records, issues late fees, follows up on delinquent payments and handles your complaints. Often, the service you receive from these companies is less than desirable since they have less invested in your business than the actual lender. You can take some steps to control the level of service you receive.

If you have complaints about your servicer, you should send a written complaint, separate from your payment, to the lender's customer service department. If they do not respond within 20 business days (as they are required to under Section 6 of the Real Estate Settlement Procedures Act [RESPA]), file a complaint with Department of Housing and Human Development (HUD) or the Consumer Protection Division of your state's attorney general's office. Don't ignore or absorb abusive practices by servicers.

You should also be aware of general predatory practices. For instance, it is now illegal for Realtors® and lenders to mark up the price of services that they don't provide, such as appraisals and credit reports. The best way to make sure you get what you are promised is to carefully review every document before signing it. You are the customer and loans are a competitive market. Be sure to demand the service you deserve.

13. finding Your Next Home

I recently sold a property in Berkeley with the professional assistance of Ira and Carol Serkes. The
reason I selected Ira and Carol to be my selling
agents was simply because I bought the same
property five years ago through them and was extremely pleased with their service. There was no
doubt in my mind that when it was time to sell, I
would be listing with Ira and Carol Serkes. I can
confidently say that Ira and Carol are knowledgeable and give sound advice. They respect the fact
that the client is the ultimate decision maker regarding every aspect of the transaction. As the negotiations proceeded (and sometime got a bit
strange), they kept me informed of every tiny detail by phone calls, faxes, and mail. If I had to buy
or sell again in the Bay Area, I am sure I would call
them right away.

—Amjad Noorani

Once you have established a relationship with your
Realtor® and have your lender on board, you can look for a
home with a much better perspective on what you can
afford. Whether you are a first-time homebuyer, looking
for a second home or building your real estate investment
portfolio, knowledge brings understanding and control to
the process. You will also be in a better position when making an offer because you are already preapproved for your
loan.

The Search

Your Realtor® will first select homes for you to see from the Multiple Listing Service (MLS). However, an agent is not limited to the MLS. They will probably be aware of new-home construction projects and might peruse the newspaper classifieds or otherwise be aware of homes being sold directly by owners. Occasionally, they may have knowledge of a home or two that the owners have not absolutely decided to sell, but who are considering it. In addition, you might see open house signs or other signs on homes that appeal to you. A word of caution: Once you have selected a Realtor® and have an agreement to work together, if you see a sign on a house for sale, *do not* call on the sign. Call your Realtor® instead and ask them to do the research, let you know the details and set a showing if it proves appropriate. Also, ask them how you should handle yourself in open houses. Keep in mind that the listing agent sitting at the open house or named on a front-lawn signpost usually represents the seller, and would like nothing more than to claim you as "their" buyer. Most agents use an open house as their "virtual office" and that is how they get new clients!

The homes selected by your Realtor® should generally encompass your stated parameters, including price range, number of bedrooms and baths, general size, garage and other physical attributes. They will be in your preferred neighborhoods, communities or school districts, and will have other characteristics you have indicated are important to you. As you look, you may find you cannot put all the things you want together in one package. You can get the home you want, but not in the right school district, and so on. You may have to refine your search several times. If you stick to the price parameters established between you, your lender, and your Realtor®, then you may have to give up some of your preferences. If you are unwilling to give anything up, then you will have to take another look at financing—bringing in a family member to cosign, working with a partner or looking for properties in which the seller will carry all, or part, of the financing.

Even if you believe that the home you are purchasing is your dream home and that you will never leave it, listen to your Realtor®'s advice about which homes will have better resale value in the future. As we mentioned, many clients have traded up to better homes, often several times more than they ever imagined.

Recently, a past client approached Ken. When this couple bought their home, they swore they would live in it for 10 years or longer—this was exactly where they wanted to be. It was less than two years later, and they wanted him to list their home for sale. They smiled when they reminded Ken what he had said when they bought, it was: "I'll bet you a thousand dollars you will not be in this home five years from now. In fact, you will probably move on in less than three years." Ken forgot that bet, but it illustrates how people's needs and desires change over time.

You can also ask how much the sellers paid, why they are selling, or about anything adverse in the neighborhood. You can't guarantee honest answers, but you will hopefully get a better understanding of whether or not this is the home you want to commit to. The bottom line is that if you have a plan, and you stick to the plan and understand your limits, you will be in a better position to stave off buyer's remorse.

There is no way to learn everything about a home before you buy it. You can learn a lot, and we will discuss some of those things here. But the neighborhood, your neighbors and future plans for the community are all factors you will discover over time. Your local government may decide to build a highway a few blocks away. Private enterprise may decide to put in a shopping center. Your job situation may change, or you may simply decide you would prefer living in another area for any variety of reasons. Very little in life is permanent. So while you may be perfectly happy with the home you choose to buy now, do not be afraid to buy if everything is not perfect.

You see, contracts simply keep everything nice and tidy. If everyone you dealt with were completely honest, had an impeccable memory, and always had it in their heart to do the right thing, contracts probably wouldn't be necessary. But even honest people have short memories, or become hurried, or decide they've already given too much, which makes contracts valuable necessities.

Bring your Realtor® with you on your walk-through. Bring to the listing agent's attention anything that wasn't completed according to the contract, and have it corrected prior to closing. Ultimately, you hold the trump card: You have the money to hand over at the closing table, and if your agreement hasn't been honored, you can decline to close. Practically speaking, that rarely happens when everything is in place to close. You've probably packed or otherwise made plans to move out of your current residence, you are excited about being in a new home and the pressure is on everyone to go ahead and sign. So again, don't sweat the small stuff.

Anything significant should be handled with a written agreement at closing, or by setting aside additional money in escrow. For example, let's say the seller was to replace the furnace but couldn't arrange for a repairperson in time. You could all agree to have the escrow company withhold that money from the proceeds due to be paid to the seller. The escrow company would then pay the repairperson when the work was complete. Or if the carpet was supposed to be cleaned but wasn't, the seller could hand you a check at closing to pay for it.

What do you do if the seller refuses? You have to make a decision. Is it more important to close, or should you walk away? We're not telling you this because it happens often, but because it does happen occasionally, it's best to be prepared.

If your transaction is typical, everything will have been completed per agreement and you'll sign the closing papers, present your check and get the keys to the house. Everybody walks away with a big grin on their face, looking forward to the new lives they have created. Now for the fun part—it's time to move in to your new home!

14. Epilogue

Samia is an excellent real estate agent who gets the job done. I was particularly impressed by her professionalism and her interpersonal skills. Samia is hard working, organized, and very meticulous. Overall, Samia did the job where other agents I tried to use had previously failed.

—Scott Hafer, United States Postal Service

Selling your home and buying a new one are two ways we have of improving our lives. Hopefully, establishing relationships with professionals who help us throughout our lives represents another means of improvement. So many of our clients have become our lifelong friends. It certainly makes this business of real estate an enjoyable occupation for us.

If you follow some of the advice presented here, we are positive that your efforts will result in similar relationships. It's often said that it can be dangerous working with a friend, and certainly many good friendships are lost once an otherwise trusted friend demonstrates any level of incompetence under the guise of service. Friend or not, you are paying for professional service that should transcend a friendship. When service does not meet expectations, friendships suffer. On the other hand, when professionalism is demonstrated first, the result can be lasting friendship.

We hope nothing less for you.

To Reach Ira & Carol Serkes
RE/MAX Executive
1758 Solano Avenue
Berkeley, CA 94707
Phone: (510) 526-6668
Toll Free (800) 887-6668
Fax: (510) 524-6869
BerkeleyHomes.com
BerkeleyRealEstate.com
Serkes@berkeleyhomes.com

To Reach Samia S.Morgan, Inc.
Keller Williams Realty
344 Landfair Avenue
San Mateo, CA 94403
Phone: (650) 352-5220
Toll-Free: (800) 493-1715
Fax: (650) 745-3999
Move2CA.com
SamiaMorgan.com
Samia@SamiaMorgan.com

To Reach Pete Sabine
RE/MAX C.C. Connection
Phone: (925) 407-0606
ContraCostaLiving.com
Pete@ContraCostaLiving.com

To Reach Ken Deshaies
P.O. PO Box 1608–265 Tanglewood Lane
Silverthorne, CO 80498
Phone: 970-262-SNOW (7669) or (888) 353-SNOW
Cell: (970) 485-1891
Fax: (866) 782-6059
www.SnowHome.com

To find out if you can become a
published author, visit:
GabrielBooks.com
or call
(800) 940-2622 Toll Free

APPENDIX A

Glossary
of
Terms

This is excerpted from the glossary included on the National Association of REALTORS® (NAR) website. Real estate brokerage is truly dependent on the "lingo," and this is only a partial list. Go to their website at www.realtor.com and click on "Real Estate Glossary" for more.

Acceleration clause A provision in a mortgage that gives the lender the right to demand payment of the entire principal balance if a monthly payment is missed.

Adjustable-rate mortgage (ARM) A mortgage that permits the lender to adjust its interest rate periodically on the basis of changes in a specified index.

Amortization The gradual repayment of a mortgage loan by installments.

Annual percentage rate (APR) The cost of a mortgage stated as a yearly rate; includes such items as interest, mortgage insurance, and loan origination fee (points).

Appraisal A written analysis of the estimated value of a property prepared by a qualified appraiser. As contrasted to a home inspection.

Assumable mortgage A mortgage that can be taken over ("assumed") by the buyer when a home is sold. Almost never seen now.

Balloon mortgage A mortgage that has level monthly payments that will amortize it over a stated term but that provides for a lump sum payment to be due at the end of an earlier specified term.

Bridge (swing) loan A form of second trust that is collateralized by the borrower's present home (which is usually for sale) in a manner that allows the proceeds to be used for closing on a new house before the present home is sold. Also known as a "swing loan."

Broker A person who, for a commission or a fee, brings parties together and assists in negotiating contracts between them.

Buydown mortgage A temporary buydown is a mortgage on which an initial lump-sum payment is made by any party to reduce a borrower's monthly payments during the first few years of a mortgage. A permanent buydown reduces the interest rate over the entire life of a mortgage.

Cap A provision of an adjustable-rate mortgage (ARM) that limits how much the interest rate or mortgage payments may increase or decrease.

Closing costs Expenses (over and above the price of the property) incurred by buyers and sellers in transferring ownership of a property. Closing costs normally include an origination fee, an attorney's fee, taxes, an amount placed in escrow, and charges for obtaining title insurance and a survey. Closing costs percentage will vary according to the area of the country; lenders or Realtors® often provide estimates of closing costs to prospective homebuyers.

Commission The fee charged by a broker or agent for negotiating a real estate or loan transaction. A commission is generally a percentage of the price of the property or loan.

Contingency A condition that must be met before a contract is legally binding. For example, home purchasers often include a contingency that specifies that the contract is not binding until the purchaser obtains a satisfactory home inspection report from a qualified home inspector.

Conventional mortgage A mortgage that is not insured or guaranteed by the federal government. Usually requires a 20 percent down payment.

Deed The legal document conveying title to a property.

Due-on-sale provision A provision in a mortgage that allows the lender to demand repayment in full if the borrower sells the property that serves as security for the mortgage.

Earnest money deposit A deposit made by the potential home buyer to show that he or she is serious about buying the house.

Easement A right of way giving persons other than the owner access to, or over, a property.

Encroachment An improvement that intrudes illegally on another's property.

Encumbrance Anything that affects or limits the fee simple title to a property, such as mortgages, leases, easements, or restrictions.

Escrow An item of value, money, or documents deposited with a third party to be delivered upon the fulfillment of a condition. For example, the deposit by a borrower with the lender of funds to pay taxes and insurance premiums when they become due, or the deposit of funds or documents with an attorney or escrow agent to be disbursed upon the closing of a sale of real estate.

Fannie Mae Fannie Mae is a New York Stock Exchange company and the largest non-bank financial services company in the world. It operates pursuant to a federal charter and is the nation's largest source of financing for home mortgages. Over the past 30 years, Fannie Mae has provided nearly $2.5 trillion of mortgage financing for over 30 million families.

Federal Housing Administration (FHA) An agency of the U.S. Department of Housing and Urban Development (HUD). Its main activity is the insuring of residential mortgage loans made by private lenders. The FHA sets standards for construction and underwriting but does not lend money or plan or construct housing.

FHA mortgage A mortgage that is insured by the Federal Housing Administration (FHA). Also known as a government mortgage. The loan is made by a private financial institution.

Fixed rate mortgage A mortgage in which the interest rate is fixed for the duration of the loan. You always know what the payments will be. Usually the interest is higher than with an ARM.

Flood insurance Insurance that compensates for physical property damage resulting from flooding. It is required for properties located in federally designated flood areas.

Hazard insurance Insurance coverage that compensates for physical damage to a property from fire, wind, vandalism, or other hazards. Does not cover personal property. It is almost always required, as a minimum, by the lender.

Home inspection A thorough inspection that evaluates the structural and mechanical condition of a home. This is not the same as an appraisal of property.

Homeowner's insurance An insurance policy that combines personal liability insurance and hazard insurance coverage for a dwelling and its contents.

HUD-1 statement A document that provides an itemized listing of the funds that are payable at closing. Items that appear on the statement include real estate commissions, loan fees, points, and initial escrow amounts. Each item on the statement is represented by a separate number within a standardized numbering system. The totals at the bottom of the HUD-1 statement define the seller's net proceeds and the buyer's net payment at closing. The blank form for the statement is published by the Department of Housing and Urban Development (HUD). The HUD-1 statement is also known as the "closing statement" or "settlement sheet."

Insured conventional loan A loan with less than 20 percent downpayment. The difference is covered by Private Mortgage Insurance (PMI). The PMI can be dropped from your monthly payments when you have established 20 percent equity in your property. You can accomplish this by your payments and the appreciated cash value of your home by qualified appraisal.

Interest rate The rate of interest in effect for the monthly payment due.

Lien A legal claim against a property that must be paid off when the property is sold.

Lock-in A written agreement in which the lender guarantees a specified interest rate if a mortgage goes to closing within a set period of time. The lock-in also usually specifies the number of points to be paid at closing.

Maturity The date on which the principal balance of a loan, bond, or other financial instrument becomes due and payable.

Mortgage A legal document that pledges a property to the lender as security for payment of a debt.

Mortgage insurance A contract that insures the lender against loss caused by a mortgager's default on a government mortgage or conventional mortgage. Mortgage insurance can be issued by a private company or by a government agency such as the Federal Housing Administration (FHA). Depending on the type of mortgage insurance, the insurance may cover a percentage of or virtually all of the mortgage loan. See private mortgage insurance (PMI).

Mortgage insurance premium (MIP) The amount paid by a mortgagor for mortgage insurance, either to a government agency such as the Federal Housing Administration (FHA) or to a private mortgage insurance (PMI) company. See private mortgage insurance below. MIP is usually a one-time charge.

Origination fee A fee paid to a lender for processing a loan application. The origination fee is stated in the form of points. One point is 1 percent of the mortgage amount.

PITI See principal, interest, taxes, and insurance (PITI).

Point A unit of measurement used for various loan charges; one point equals 1 percent of the amount of the loan.

Prepayment Any amount paid to reduce the principal balance of a loan before the due date. Payment in full on a mortgage that may result from a sale of the property, the owner's decision to pay off the loan in full, or a fore-closure. In each case, prepayment means payment occurs before the loan has been fully amortized.

Prequalification The process of determining how much money a prospective home buyer will be eligible to borrow before he or she applies for a loan.

Principal, interest, taxes, and insurance (PITI) The four components of a monthly mortgage payment. Prin-cipal refers to the part of the monthly payment that reduces the remaining balance of the mortgage. Interest is the fee charged for borrowing money. Taxes and insur-ance refer to the amounts that are paid into an escrow account each month for property taxes and mortgage and hazard insurance.

Private mortgage insurance (PMI) Mortgage insur-ance that is provided by a private mortgage insurance company to protect lenders against loss if a borrower defaults. Most lenders generally require PMI for a loan with a loan-to-value (LTV) percentage in excess of 80 per-cent. This is a recurring monthly charge, reflected in the PITI.

Qualifying ratios Calculations that are used in deter-mining whether a borrower can qualify for a mortgage. They consist of two separate calculations: a housing expense as a percent of income ratio and total debt obligations as a percent of income ratio.

Realtor® A real estate broker or an associate who holds active membership in a local real estate board that is affiliated with the National Association of REALTORS®.

Right of first refusal A provision in an agreement that requires the owner of a property to give another party the first opportunity to purchase or lease the property before he or she offers it for sale or lease to others.

Second mortgage A mortgage that has a lien position subordinate to the first mortgage.

Settlement sheet See HUD-1 statement.

Title A legal document evidencing a person's right to or ownership of a property.

Title insurance Insurance that protects the lender (lender's policy) or the buyer (owner's policy) against loss arising from disputes over ownership of a property.

Underwriting The process of evaluating a loan application to determine the risk involved for the lender. Underwriting involves an analysis of the borrower's creditworthiness and the quality of the property itself.

VA mortgage A mortgage that is guaranteed by the Department of Veterans Affairs (VA). Also known as a government mortgage. The loan is made by a private financial institution.

APPENDIX B

Home Preparation Checklist

Step 1: Make Any Needed Repairs to the Primary Systems and Components of Your Home

(Unless you are selling your home "as is", buyers will need to know that your home's systems are in working order. If they are not, you should make the repairs before putting your home on the market unless you want to compensate the buyer monetarily. Take a thorough inventory and inspection of the following systems and components of your home to make sure that they are in working order. While these repairs might be costly, it will usually save you money to take care of them now rather than crediting the buyer at closing. These are items that you need to repair before you do anything else to your home if you can handle the expense).

❏ Make sure that your roof is in good repair. If your home has been experiencing any leaks, your roof might need to be replaced. If any shingles are loose or broken, they need to be replaced.

❏ Check to see that your rain gutters are flowing properly and in the right direction and are free of leaves and dirt.

❏ Your heating and air conditioning should be in good working order. If they are not, this can definitely cause problems in finding buyers for your house.

❏ Make sure that your house is structurally sound. Any cracks in the walls or ceilings should be filled in immediately to avoid further cracking.

❏ Check that all plumbing and septic systems are working as they should. If they are not, call in a plumber or other specialists as needed.

❏ Check your house for termites or any other pests. If you find any, call in a specialist to get rid of them!

❑ If your home has mold you should take care of it unless you are willing to sell your home for less or possibly not even find a buyer.

❑ Check your home for flood damage if you live in an area where flooding could be a problem.

❑ Radon and lead paint are serious problems that you should check for. It is best to know now rather than be surprised later on and have a deal fall through.

❑ If you have any broken windows, window panes, screens or doors, you should pay to have them fixed.

❑ If you have any broken appliances that are fixtures and therefore will be included in the sale, such as the dishwasher, you should pay to have them fixed or replaced. Likewise, repair any broken light fixtures.

❑ If you have a gas stove, make sure that it works properly and that there are no gas leaks.

❑ Make sure all electrical systems are working properly. This includes any electrical gates, garage, doorbell, intercom, and so on.

❑ If there are any dead or "sick" trees on your property, have them cut down.

Step 2: The Exterior of Your Home

(The exterior of your house is the first thing a potential buyer will see as they approach. Make sure that it looks neat and cared for. Use the following checklist as a guide.)

❑ Your lawn should be mowed and well trimmed. An overgrown lawn can be a big turn off to potential buyers and can really detract their attention from other aspects of your home.

❑ Your lawn should also be green and not brown. Fertilize it if necessary and remember to keep it free of weeds.

❑ Shrubs, flowers, trees and bushes should be well trimmed and healthy looking. Let buyers know that you care for your home lovingly. Well cared for greenery can give your home much added appeal.

❑ If you have fruit trees, make sure to get rid of any rotting fruit that has fallen to the ground.

❑ Rake your lawn and front drive free of drifting leaves.

❑ Make sure that your front walk, lawn and entryway are clear of clutter. Get rid of any toys or bikes and store them properly.

❑ Hose down your front entryway so it is clean and free of dirt. If it is stained, think about covering the stain with a nice doormat if it can't be cleaned.

❑ If your driveway has any oil stains, clean them. Oil stains can really be an eye sore.

❑ If your front door looks old or worn, give it a fresh coat of paint or polish it.

❑ Think about placing some potted flowers by your front door. Flowers always look pretty and smell sweet.

❑ Wash your windows!

❑ If you haven't painted your house in some time and it is looking a bit shabby, you might want to consider painting it, but try to stay away from bold colors.

❑ Fix or replace any broken shutters, shingles or bricks.

Step 3: The Interior of Your Home

(Most of the steps taken here will be more time intensive than anything else so follow these steps to make the inside of your home attractive and inviting).

❏ Organize and minimize everything in your home from top to bottom. This will involve going through every room, closet, cabinet and any other storage area such as the garage and clearing out your belongings. You want to let potential buyers see as much clear space as possible so this is the time to get rid of anything you no longer want or need and store the rest of your belongings neatly. You will have to do this eventually when you move, so why not start now in order to help give your home some added appeal to potential buyers? If you have so much stuff that you don't know what to do with it all, consider storing it with family or friends or perhaps renting storage space.

❏ Make sure that your house is clean and tidy. Clean everything in your house inside and out. Wax the floors, make sure the walls are free of dirt and smudges and dust and vacuum your furniture.

❏ Go through every room in your house and make sure that the furniture is arranged to make the room look the most spacious and aesthetically pleasing. Enlist the opinions of others. If you have torn, broken, very worn out or dirty furniture, you should get rid of it if you plan to do so anyway. If you can't, try covering the furniture. For example, a nice afghan over an old couch can do the trick.

❏ Make sure that the parts of your home that you like best are getting good lighting. Make sure that the windows are unobstructed to let in the sunlight and keep the curtains or blinds open.

❏ Wash the windows so they are completely clear. If any window coverings are worn or broken, fix or replace them.

❏ Make sure that all of your lights are working. Replace burned-out bulbs, but make sure to keep the lighting inviting.

❏ Clean your kitchen counters and tile so they sparkle and clean the sink. Kitchens are very important to buyers so make sure that yours is clean and bright. The kitchen is also a great place to place fresh flowers.

❏ Clean everything in the bathroom until it shines. Get rid of any rust stains. Hang fresh, clean towels neatly.

❏ Air out your house to get rid of any bad or stale odors. Try to bring in some fresh scents with flowers or a touch of vanilla.

Step 4: Updating Your Home

(If you have the time and the money, there are certain things that you can do to your home to give it added appeal and a much better selling price. There are certain things that buyers look for when buying a home, so if you do have the means, consider the following projects if they are needed).

❏ Remodels and updates in the kitchen are where you can get the greatest returns on your investment when you sell your home. If your kitchen is outdated and you have the means, certain updates can greatly improve your chances at selling your home for a better price.

❏ If your appliances are over 10 years old, replace them with new, modern appliances. Stainless steel appliances are the latest trends today.

❑ Old cabinets and countertops can also be replaced. If you are handy, this can even be a do-it-yourself project. Natural woods for the cabinets and granite or tile countertops can make your kitchen sparkle.

❑ Old linoleum flooring in the kitchen can really make the room look dingy. Consider replacing with hardwood or even tile.

❑ After the kitchen, updates in the bathroom are where you will see a good return on your investment in the sale price of your home. Buyers today are looking for modern bathrooms with all the latest conveniences. Glass shower doors, new tiles, flooring and new fixtures can all give your bathrooms an entirely new look.

❑ If your walls are looking dirty and old, a new paint job can do wonders to the look of the inside of your home. This can be an inexpensive project that can really brighten up the rooms of your house. Choose neutral colors for a warm and soft look that will appeal to the greatest number of buyers.

❑ If your floors are worn and dirty, consider replacing them. Old and worn carpeting can really detract a buyer's attention from other features of your home. New carpeting can be relatively inexpensive compared with the greater return that can be obtained in the selling price of your home.

❑ Outdated flooring such as linoleum can make your house look retro. Most buyers are looking for homes with modern updates. If you can't afford hardwood, consider vinyl.

❑ Other areas to consider are very old windows and doors. Windows encompass a great deal of your home's exterior and are definitely something that buyers will notice right away.

Congratulations, after having followed these steps and preparing your house so that it looks its best, you are now ready to sell your home!

APPENDIX C

Moving Checklist

8 Weeks Before Moving

❑ Create a "move file" to keep track of estimates, receipts and other important information.

❑ Check with the IRS to see what expenses can be deducted on your next tax return.

❑ Start pulling together medical and dental records and ask your healthcare providers for referrals in your new city.

❑ Start researching your new community. The Internet is a great resource for finding chambers of commerce and community guides.

❑ Get estimates from several moving companies and compare them.

❑ Arrange to have school records transferred to your children's new school.

6 Weeks Before Moving

❑ Make a list of things that are valuable or difficult to replace. Plan on shipping these by certified mail or carrying them with you.

❑ Start working your way through each room taking inventory and planning what to get rid of. Start planning a yard sale and find local charities.

❑ Choose a moving company and reserve the date of your move.

❑ Start collecting boxes and other packing supplies.

❑ Check how to obtain new driver's licenses and license plates.

4 Weeks Before Moving

❑ Send out change of address cards to post office, friends, subscriptions and credit cards.

❑ Hold your garage sale. Donate left over items to charity.

❑ Contact utility companies and notify them of disconnect dates. Arrange for utility service in your new home.

❑ Start packing items you don't use often.

2 Weeks Before Moving

❑ Contact your bank and/or credit union to transfer or close accounts. Clear out safety deposit boxes.

❑ Confirm travel and moving arrangements.

❑ Return library books or anything borrowed from friends or neighbors.

1 Week Before Moving

❑ Finish packing! Separate essential items that you will be taking with you.

❑ Empty, defrost and clean your refrigerator at least 24 hours prior to moving day.

❑ Cancel deliveries and services such as newspapers and trash collection.

❑ Drain oil and gasoline from power equipment.

Moving Day

❑ Before the movers leave, check every room, closet and cabinet one last time.

❑ Upon arriving, inspect everything and make sure nothing was damaged during the move.

❑ Keep all moving receipts and documentation in your file.

After the Move

❑ If needed, childproof your new home.

❑ Test security and smoke alarms.

❑ Set up all appliances.

❑ Get local emergency numbers and post them.

❑ Change the locks on all doors.

❑ Explore your new neighborhood!